"Information through Innovation"

A S / 4 0 0

Using the AS/400

An Introduction

A S / 4 0 0

Patrice Gapen

Catherine Stoughton

Laramie County Community College

bf

boyd & fraser publishing company

Dedication
—

To Rod, who washed dishes, folded laundry, and took care of the children so I had time to write. P.G.

To Herb and Sean, Thanks so much for your support. C.S.

Credits
—

Senior Acquisitions Editor: James H. Edwards
Production Coordinator: Patty Stephan
Interior Design: Designworks
Cover Design: Mike Fender Design
Composition: Rebecca Evans & Associates

 © 1993 boyd & fraser publishing company
A Division of South-Western Publishing Company
Danvers, MA 01923

Manufactured in the United States of America.

Names of all products mentioned herein are used for identification purposes only and may be trademarks of their respective owners. South-Western Publishing Company and boyd & fraser publishing company disclaim any affiliation, association, or connection with, or sponsorship or endorsement by such owners.

Library of Congress Cataloging-in-Publication Data
Gapen, Patrice.
    Using the AS/400: an introduction / by Patrice Gapen, Catherine Stoughton.
        p.   cm.
    Includes index.
    ISBN 0–87835–952–4
    1. IBM AS/400 (Computer)   I. Stoughton, Catherine.   II. Title.
QA76.8.I25919G36   1992
004.1′45—dc20   92-22205
                                                                  CIP

1 2 3 4 5 6 7 8 9 H 4 3 2

CONTENTS

PREFACE

To the Instructor

The AS/400 learning curve is steep because there are a variety of methods for accomplishing the same task. This complicates both learning the system and instructing on this platform. *Using the AS/400: An Introduction* is intended to simplify these activities. It is designed for an introductory course preceding programming languages, or as an introduction to hardware and software for operator trainee courses.

Using the AS/400: An Introduction focuses on the most fundamental and important menu options. Concepts that are constant throughout the software are presented and terminology has been shortened and simplified. Therefore the advanced user or system administrator will notice some details that are not "technically" correct. For instance, the more familiar term "file" is used throughout the text, whereas the more proper term is "database file."

New material is initially introduced through a series of menus whenever possible. Walking students step by step through the layers of menus aids in long-term absorption. The Control Language (CL) command, which bypasses the menus and executes the same or similar functions as the menus, is introduced through TIPS. While the goal is for the student to use CL commands as quickly as possible, the authors feel that this combination of approaches will meet the needs of the novice as well as the computer professional who is upgrading to this hardware.

One library with the same name as the student's userid has been chosen. One source physical file object, SOURCE, will be used to store all DDS, Query, RPG, and COBOL source code. This approach was chosen for simplicity, as the complexity and terminology of the AS/400 are already overwhelming to the beginning student. For the first-time AS/400 user, it is much easier to deal with only one source physical file. When students have mastered the concepts, adding another source physical file is a relatively minor endeavor. Students themselves can create a new source physical file, which aids in understanding how the production environment would utilize separate objects. Classes in the individual languages may include creation of a source physical file for each of the different languages.

A clear understanding of objects, libraries, and members makes the use of the PDM (Programming Development Manager) menus a good starting place, and many organizations use only PDM. The authors also envision teaching students to use the Programmer's menu once mastery of PDM is achieved. Student exposure to PDM is mandatory for both of these reasons.

This text is based on Version 2 Release 1 Modification 0 of the operating system. The Instructor's Manual, available free to adopting instructors, contains the CL source code to create the student environment objects referred to in this text. These objects include the user profile, job description, SOURCE physical file, and output queue.

PREFACE

To the Student

This introductory book was written to help you learn how to use the IBM AS/400. There is usually more than one way to get to a particular screen, menu, or function on the AS/400, and this can often be perplexing. Initially, the text shows how to use the series of menus (called menu chaining) that is required for a given task. After you are comfortable with the menu chaining concept, a more efficient method of completing the task, which will replace the menus, may be introduced.

AS/400 menu chaining can be likened to a series of descending staircases. Each staircase has a different number of steps and leads the user to a different location within the operating system. Locating the proper staircase and descending the appropriate number of steps can initially be confusing. To make the learning process easier, *Using the AS/400: An Introduction* first provides an overview of the material in each section. Then a series of menus is displayed that leads to the proper "staircase," and each "stair" is explained as you descend deeper into the operating system.

Periodically, the Control Language (CL) command method is presented as an alternative to menu chaining. The Control Language (CL) command is more efficient, and is presented through a series of TIPS. TIPS show the CL command that selects both the "staircase" and the "step" needed for a given operation. You may continue to use menu chaining, or you can use the CL command. In many cases, students choose to use a combination of both methods. Transition to the CL commands can be made as soon as you are comfortable with them.

Acknowledgments

The authors would like to thank the following reviewers, whose comments served to enhance the quality of the manuscript.

Jerry Fottral
Kirkwood Community College

Michael J. Ryan
Lansing Community College

John Hoffman
Milwaukee Area Technical College

Norman Seaton
El Centro College

Carol Jones
Isothermal Community College

Ted Simpson
Wisconsin Indianhead Technical College

Blanca Moore
Champlain College

Ted Tucker
Metropolitan Community College

Ken Morganstern
North County Tech

David Wen
Diablo Valley College

Joan Roberts
Front Range Community College

Judy Yeager
Western Michigan University

Thanks are also due to Mark Mercer of Unicover Corporation and Steve Gaumond of Twinstar, Inc. for their continued encouragement and assistance.

The AS/400 Operating Environment

To describe the hardware available on the AS/400.

To understand the AS/400 working environment.

To describe the systems and application software available on the AS/400.

INTRODUCTION

Most workers are familiar with personal computers, as they are now a standard tool in the business world. The personal computer is just that: a tool dedicated to one person at a time. Larger computers, known as mainframes and midrange computers, also have their place in the business world. As a business grows, the need to have shared information (databases) becomes more and more important. Any computer that can do multiple tasks at the same time is referred to as a "multi-user" computer.

Try to imagine a large mail-order company that did not have the ability to share computerized files. The ordering department staff would not know a customer's credit limit, nor would it know what items were currently out of stock. This company would not last long in the competitive marketplace. Now imagine that this same company was computerized but that only one person could use the customer files at a time. While one clerk was taking an order, the shipping department would have to wait before printing mailing labels. If the payroll department was calculating payroll, no customer orders could be entered into the computer. This would be a disastrous situation.

Some computers have each type of information isolated into separate files. In the mail-order company, the product number, description, cost to the customer, and quantity on hand might be in one file. Another file might contain the vendor that supplies the product, the vendor's address and phone number, and the product cost. Joining these two files would not be an easy task in a traditional system. The company would also not want customers to know the markup on products. The company would be concerned that the product cost be kept confidential.

Security and joining data from multiple files are very difficult on traditional mainframe, mini, and personal computers but not on the AS/400 computer. The IBM Application System/400 (AS/400) represents IBM's midrange business computing system. The AS/400 solves the need for many people to use the same data at the same time, as it is a multiple-user midrange computer system. One AS/400 can support from four to over 500 active users. This computer was designed for a multiple-user environment, so substantial security is built into the operating system. Users and application developers can work side by side and never interfere with each other's work. The AS/400 also keeps all of the data files in a database format. This format allows for ease of merging multiple types of data from many sources.

The AS/400 consists of a family of compatible models that utilize the same operating system. This provides consistent programmer and end-user interfaces for businesses of all sizes and allows for a steady growth without major changes in hardware. A wide variety of connectivity options are provided to allow data communications within the AS/400 family and to other IBM systems and personal computers.

Some businesses purchase their AS/400 application software, while others hire programmers to develop software for them. In either case the end-users have access to customized selections from menus designed with their needs in mind. To use the new features available on the AS/400, considerable knowledge about this computer is essential. The AS/400 is not a microcomputer (PC) and does not operate like one. It is controlled by an IBM-developed proprietary operating system. The OS/400 operating system is unlike other common PC or mainframe operating systems.

The IBM AS/400 is a new computer system based on the concepts developed with the older IBM System/36 and IBM System/38 minicomputers. The AS/400 can be configured to emulate either of these operating environments. Emulation in these different environments allows a business to purchase the new hardware but still operate with the existing (old) software. The dual nature of these environments allows a slower and more methodical conversion to the newer programming methods that are available only on the AS/400. However, this text will discuss only the OS/400 operating system and is not intended to be a conversion guide from the S/36 or S/38, nor will emulation techniques be discussed.

Another trend in the industry is to cut computer center costs and thereby have a more competitive company by downsizing from an IBM mainframe to an AS/400. This trend will continue, since the AS/400 architecture is more similar to a mainframe than to any other type of existing platform. The AS/400 also offers the advantages of the integrated relational database and more programmer productivity software.

AS/400 HARDWARE

Processor and Storage

The AS/400 hardware consists of a processor, at least one permanent storage device, one or more display stations, and one or more printers. Larger models offer multiple processors to increase processing capacity. The smallest model is smaller than a two-drawer file cabinet, and the largest processor fits into a walk-in closet. Main memory ranges from 8 megabytes to over 500 megabytes, and fixed disk storage ranges from 640 megabytes to over 123 gigabytes. Auxiliary storage also includes a variety of sizes of magnetic tape, 5.25-inch or 8.00-inch diskettes, and optical disk storage. See Figure 1.1 for the IBM AS/400 Product Family.

Connectivity

The AS/400 supports connectivity to local and/or remote display stations and printers. The AS/400 can also communicate to IBM mainframes as well as microcomputers. This computer supports a variety of protocols and networks, including IBM Token-Ring Network, Ethernet, Asynchronous, Binary Synchronous, Synchronous, ISDN, SNA, and TCP/IP.

Display Station and PC Screens

The AS/400 supports display stations (dumb terminals) and the PS/2 microcomputer (or any IBM-compatible PC). These devices will respond in the same way when you are on the AS/400, but they usually have different keyboards.

The monitor displays menus and output. Menu screens will have function key options and can have command line options. A command line will appear near the bottom of the screen. There is also an indicator line at the bottom of every screen (the last line). The indicator line can display waiting message and input inhibit indicators. The input inhibit indicator (an "X" on a display station and "II" highlighted on a PC) tells the user that the keyboard is locked and no input will be accepted. This occurs if the system is busy processing input and cannot accept more input from you. The input inhibit indicator will disappear when the system has completed the task and is ready for more information.

If you have one or more messages in your message queue, you will have a message waiting symbol (a "torn corner" graphic on the display station and "MW" highlighted on a PC).

Refer to the Display Station manual for additional information on either of these topics.

Display Station and PC Keyboards
—

The display station keyboard has 122 keys (see Figure 1.2), many of which will be unfamiliar to a microcomputer user. In using the PC as the display station (see Figure 1.3), the microcomputer control keys have different meanings. You will have to become familiar with the keyboards, since pressing the wrong key can have disastrous effects.

There are two kinds of function keys on a keyboard: numbered function keys and named function keys. The display station has 24 numbered function keys (labeled F1

FIGURE 1.1   *AS/400 Family*

D80

D70

D60

D50

D45

D35

9406 Models

D04

D06

9402 Models

D25

D20

D10

9404 Models

through F24), while the PC has only 12. On a PC, to use the F13 through F24 keys, press and hold the Shift key and press the function key that when added to 12 will result in the correct key. For example, Shift/F1 is used for F13, and Shift/F8 is used for F20.

Each function key has different usages depending on the application. The operating system has attempted to standardize the function keys' usage. F3 is reserved for exiting the entire process, while F12 will cancel only the current step. F4, the prompt key, deserves special attention. When F4 is pressed after a command has been

FIGURE 1.2   *Terminal-type Keyboard*

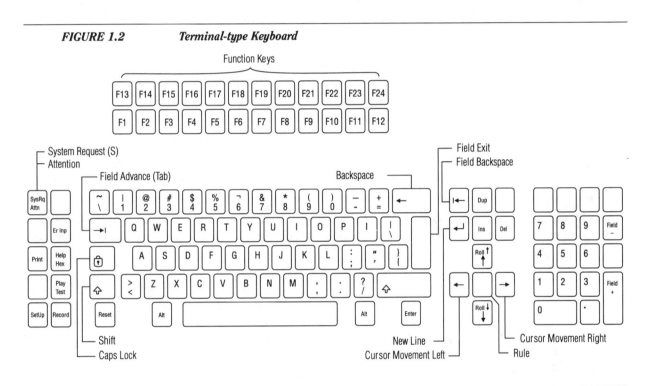

FIGURE 1.3   *PC Keyboard*

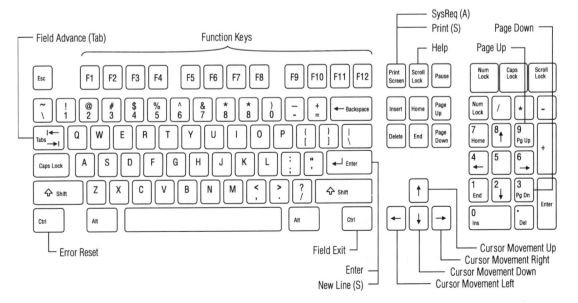

entered on the command line, all the parameters that are available for that command will be displayed. The new user and the experienced user of the AS/400 operating system will find this function key invaluable.

The named function keys have words, abbreviations of words, or symbols printed on them instead of numbers. They usually perform the functions that the words or symbols indicate, such as Print. However, if you are using a PC keyboard, these PC named function keys take on new meanings. Table 1.1 gives a brief explanation of the named function keys that you will be using most often, which are different from the functions on the PC keyboard. For an explanation of every key, refer to an IBM AS/400 manual (New User's Guide or a display station user's guide).

The PC keyboard definition used in this text is the standard default keyboard mapping when connecting an IBM PS/2 to the AS/400 with twinaxial cable and PC Support. If your installation utilizes another type of connection, see your instructor for other keyboard mapping information.

THE AS/400 WORKING ENVIRONMENT

Security

The AS/400 security functions give the person in charge of security, the Security Officer, techniques to control access to the system devices, data, and programs. Security is used to ensure that only people who have been given the authority can use these resources. Authority on the AS/400 is defined as the right to use an object, such as a data file.

The system is always checking for and verifying a user's authority to an object. Users can be given special authority to system commands, such as would be needed by operators or the Security Officer. Users can also be given specific, private authority to a particular object to allow specific operations on an object, such as moving or renaming it. Another example of specific authority to an object would be to perform operations on that object, such as reading, adding, updating, or deleting records in a data file.

When you are working on the AS/400 in the following chapters, the displays that you see may differ in sequence or appearance from those shown in this text. This is because your system security level and user profile are set up differently. As an AS/400 user, your working environment will depend upon these two items.

The security level for one AS/400 system is the same for all users of that system. The computer is shipped with Level 10, which is minimum security. The Security Officer will leave the system at Level 10 or set the security level to a higher level that provides more security. This text was created by using an AS/400 with security set to Level 30. Figure 1.4 shows the four levels of security that are available.

Your user profile is created for you by the Security Officer. The AS/400 uses the values assigned to you to control your environment when you are working on the computer. The user profile tells the AS/400 what operations are authorized and the objects that the user is allowed to access. The profile contains a user name (userid), a password, a current library name, an output queue name, and many other pieces of

TABLE 1.1	*Comparison of Keyboards*	
	DISPLAY STATION KEYBOARD:	**PC KEYBOARD:**
CAPS LOCK VS SHIFT LOCK KEY	There is no Caps Lock key. The Shift Lock key (looks like a padlock) puts the entire keyboard in uppercase. The number keys are also changed. The Caps Lock key is not a toggle key. The Caps Lock key will not reset the keyboard to lowercase (as on a PC keyboard) if you press it. You must press Shift/Reset.	The Caps Lock key puts only the alphabetic keys in uppercase. It is a toggle key and will reset the keyboard to lowercase when pressed. There is no Shift Lock key.
ENTER KEY	The Enter key works as usual. However, the numeric keypad Field Plus key is not an Enter key.	The Enter key works as usual; however, it is in a different position on this keyboard than on the display station keyboard. Be careful if you switch between keyboards!
FIELD EXIT KEY	The Field Exit key moves the cursor to the next field, but any characters at and to the right of the cursor in the field where you were typing are deleted. Therefore DO NOT USE THIS KEY TO MOVE FROM A FILLED FIELD TO ANOTHER FIELD! Use the New Line key or the Tab key for this movement.	The Field Exit key is the right Ctrl key. Field Exit moves the cursor to the next field, but any characters at and to the right of the cursor in the field where you were typing are deleted.
FIELD PLUS AND MINUS KEYS	The Field Plus and Minus keys vary by keyboard and by system. See the Display Station User Guide for additional information.	The Field Plus and Minus keys vary by keyboard and by system. See the keyboard mapping information for additional information.
HELP KEY	The Help key activates the AS/400 online Help.	The Help key is the F1 or Scroll Lock (Break) key.
NEW LINE KEY	The New Line key moves the cursor to the next input field in the next line. The New Line key is located in the group of named function keys between the standard keyboard and the numeric keypad. The New Line key is the bent left arrow key to the left of the Insert key.	The New Line key is the combination Shift/Enter keys. BE CAREFUL to press and hold the Shift and then press the Enter key! This combination of keys moves the cursor to the next input field in the next line.
PRINT KEY	The Print key sends a copy of the current display screen to the output queue, and it can be sent to the printer at a later time. A message will be shown that this has occurred, and the keyboard will be locked. You will need to press the Reset key to unlock the keyboard.	The Print key is the combination Shift/Print Screen keys. Hold the Shift key and press the Print Screen key. This sends a copy of the current display screen to the output queue. You will need to press the Reset key (left Ctrl key) to unlock the keyboard.
RESET KEY	The Reset key is used to correct or reset a keyboard error. You can often lock the keyboard by pressing a wrong key, or certain messages will lock the keyboard. Press this key to unlock the keyboard.	The Reset key is the lower left Ctrl key. The Reset key is used to correct or reset a keyboard error.
SHIFT/ROLL (PAGE UP/ DOWN) KEYS	The combination Shift/Up Arrow keys (Shift/Roll Up) causes a display that has "More..." or "+" on the lower right edge of the screen to show the next screen of data. The combination Shift/Down Arrow keys (Shift/Roll Down) causes the previous screen to be displayed.	The Shift/Roll Up occurs with the Page Down key. The Shift/Roll Down occurs with the Page Up key.

information that control your use of the AS/400. The command DSPUSRPRF can be used to look at the information in your user profile.

A user's access can be restricted immediately upon signing on to the AS/400 by the values in the "initial program to call" and "initial menu" parameters. These can force a user to access only an application program or a certain menu when signing on to the system. Depending on another system parameter's value, a user might not be able to change this initial program or menu, as the user would also have no access to a command line. This concept would normally be used for an organization's users, not computer operators or programmers.

Each user is assigned a user class. This parameter controls options that are shown on menus. The possible values, in order from lowest to highest authority, are user, programmer, system operator, security administrator, and security officer. For this text, you are assumed to have a programmer user class but not the special authority to perform system saves or job control. You will therefore notice that you can access many system menus but will receive an error message of "not authorized to access" when you try to select an option to perform a save/restore or job operation.

The security on the AS/400 is built into the operating system; it is not added on. With the system set to Level 30, no one can access the AS/400 without knowing a valid userid and a user-defined password. Therefore the only way for security to be breached on this computer is for users to give away these security codes.

Objects, Libraries, and Members

When you create anything on the AS/400, it is called an object. All of your objects are stored within your library. Your library is a system object that serves as a directory, or index, to other objects. The authors of this text assume that you will be working in a library that has the same name as your userid. This library will be your current library. On the display screen, the value *CURLIB means current library.

Your library was created by the Security Officer. Your library is defined in your user profile as the current library. If a user does not specify a library name when accessing an object, the operating system searches for the object in the libraries found in the library list. The library list contains four parts: system libraries, licensed

---

FIGURE 1.4   *Security Levels*

LEVEL 10:   This is the lowest level of security, and anyone is allowed to sign on. The system creates a user profile for each new user, and users can access all objects on the computer.

LEVEL 20:   The Security Officer must have created user profiles for each user when the system is set to Level 20. Users have the ability to access all objects on the computer.

LEVEL 30:   At this level, the Security Officer must have created user profiles for each user. However, access to objects is restricted without prior Security Officer authorization.

LEVEL 40:   This is the highest level of security. The authorization to objects is more restrictive than with Level 30.

program libraries, the current library, and user libraries. Your current library is the first user library that is searched when you request an object.

The objects within your library can be source code files, machine-executable code, file descriptions, data files, and so on. Some objects can have members, depending on the type of object they represent. There will be further discussion of objects, libraries, and members throughout this text.

OS/400 OPERATING SYSTEM SOFTWARE

Introduction

All computer systems need operating system software. System software is the interface between a user and the hardware. The OS/400 provides the tools for a user to work on the AS/400. The major functions of OS/400 include the commands to work with the system, known as Control Language commands; the ability to define and use data files; the ability to control the many jobs running on a multi-user system; programmer support; operator functions; communications support; and security.

Control Language

The operating system uses menus or commands to assist users in doing their work. Menu options or simple Control Language (CL) commands can be entered to go directly to a particular menu. OS/400 uses a default-based menu and command prompting scheme to aid users in selecting optional parameters for CL commands. The assigned default is the best guess to meet a user's needs. Defaults will change depending on a user's previous selections and the command that is being utilized.

Programs can also be written in the CL language. A CL program can be used to run a series of application programs and to act as a front-end processor for other programs. CL programs are similar to DOS batch commands. CL programs are also written for menu processing.

Work Management

The operating system uses queues to store jobs, printer output, and messages. A queue is a holding area in the form of a list. Items placed into a queue receive service in the same order as they are placed into the list (assuming that the priorities of all the items are the same). An output queue is a list of output files waiting to be printed. Reports are created as spooled files and placed into an output queue. An operator or user can specify files from the list to be printed.

A message queue is a mailbox for messages. A user receives system messages, job messages, and messages from other users. These messages can be read, replied to if necessary, and deleted when no longer needed.

A batch job is submitted to a job queue by a user, and then the user is free to do other work on the system. A college would print grade reports as a batch job, as there would be no need for any interaction between the user and the computer once the job was placed into a job queue. The computer would begin processing the grade report program as soon as it finished any jobs that were placed into the queue earlier.

Jobs can be either interactive or batch. An interactive job is a communication between a display station user and the computer. When you sign on to the AS/400, you have started an interactive session. A dialogue between an application program and a user is an interactive job, such as an online update of a student master file during college registration. Interactive jobs are not submitted to a job queue.

Subsystems

All jobs, whether interactive or batch, are run in an OS/400 subsystem. A subsystem creates a suitable environment for a job to do its work. Each subsystem allocates main storage and other system resources to enable a job to load and execute (run to completion). A subsystem also provides a priority, which determines how the job will be treated when competing for resources with other jobs within the same subsystem.

The AS/400 can contain one or many subsystems. Subsystems can be created to lock other users out of particular programs, thus enhancing security. As the number of jobs increases on the computer, more subsystems can be defined to manage those jobs. Interactive jobs could be run in one subsystem, all batch jobs in another, system operator jobs in a third, and so on. One subsystem could be set to automatically begin at 5:00 P.M. to run the evening batch jobs. Subsystems can be started and ended individually, making it easier to control the computer system.

OS/400 APPLICATION SOFTWARE

Languages

The AS/400 supports most of the popular application development programming languages, including the procedural languages BASIC/400, C/400, COBOL/400, FORTRAN/400, Pascal/400, and RPG/400. (In the remaining references to languages, the "/400" may be assumed.) The AS/400 also supports its own problem-oriented language, Query/400, and a database retrieval language, SQL. In addition, another language called Control Language (CL) is provided for performing operating system tasks. CL can be used for a single operating system request or to create complex programs that present the user with menus and begin other application programs.

Any programming language source code is known as a source member on the AS/400. Source members will be stored within a source physical file object within a library. These source members will need to be compiled, as do all procedural programming languages on all computers. The resulting machine language object is also placed within your library.

Database Management System

The built-in relational database management system allows data to be available to all users. Files and record definitions can be externally described on the AS/400. File and record definitions do not need to reside within an application program. Therefore programs written in any language can use the same definition. This also improves programmer productivity because the database definition is an installation standard.

A physical file is a description of the data as it is stored on the AS/400. A physical file is an object of type *FILE. A physical file contains a record format and contains one or more members. A physical file member usually contains the data records, although there can be empty physical files. A physical file is designed to simulate a traditional file.

A logical file on the AS/400 never contains any data because it references one or more physical files. A logical file could be a partial view of the actual data or one or more keys to access the physical data in a different sequence. A logical file allows the user to view the information stored in one or more files in a different sequence without duplicating the data. Assume that a physical file is in customer number sequence. However, the marketing manager wishes to view the sales figures by territory. A logical file could be developed that would allow access of the data by territory.

Screen Design Aid

Screen Design Aid (SDA) is an AS/400 Application Development Tool used to design menus and display screens. SDA generates Data Description Specifications (DDS). These externally defined specifications can then be used by any AS/400 high-level application programming language.

The programmer does not need to have extensive Data Description Specification knowledge to utilize SDA. The display is created interactively so that what is being designed and changed is visible. When a display screen is designed, fields can be selected from existing database files. Displays can be tested with actual data before being used in a high-level language program.

Menus can be easily created with SDA. Each menu option becomes a call to an AS/400 program. A program can be coded with help text to aid the operator or user. Pop-up windows can also be created for menus to aid users in more complex tasks.

A major advantage to using SDA is that programming languages need only use the input and output variables defined on the menu and display screens. The programming languages do not need to be concerned about the physical placement of the variables on the screen, screen headings or titles, color, protected fields, and so on. Screen Design Aid allows these functions to be done independently of the language. The languages need only read and write the menu and displays to a workstation. See the AS/400 Screen Design Aid manual for more information.

PC Support/400

PC Support/400 is an IBM-licensed program that provides additional system functions to any PC attached to the AS/400. Microcomputers use a coding system called ASCII. The AS/400 uses an EBCDIC coding system. This coding system determines how characters are compared and sorted. To translate the EBCDIC to ASCII requires a PC to have an emulator board. This is necessary in the PC to send and receive EBCDIC, and PC Support is the communication software.

PC Support adds other functions to this communication connection. PC Support is a set of programs that allow a user to store PC data on the AS/400 so that other users can share it, use printers attached to the AS/400 as PC printers, run PC commands while in an interactive AS/400 session, upload PC data to the AS/400, and download AS/400 data to a PC.

The uploading of ASCII data to the AS/400 is a very powerful and useful feature. Programmers can key in source code members, such as COBOL or BASIC, on any PC, and do not have to tie up system resources. Users can transfer data files from popular PC spreadsheet and database packages to the AS/400 to be processed. This eliminates rekeying data, saving time and increasing accuracy.

Downloading data from the AS/400 is the reverse of uploading. The EBCDIC data can be downloaded to a PC spreadsheet, and program source code can be easily moved to ASCII computers.

OfficeVision/400

OfficeVision/400 is an IBM-licensed product that provides office functions to AS/400 users. OfficeVision provides full word processing capabilities, including a spelling checker. A proofreading aid is also available to flag words that are beyond a specified reading level, from grades 4 through 16. Documents can also be managed within a document library, where AS/400 security can limit access to specific documents within a folder. A folder is a directory of OfficeVision documents.

OfficeVision is also an office task manager, as it includes an option to send and receive mail. The electronic mail feature provides the ability to send short messages or full documents to one or many users.

A third feature of OfficeVision is calendars. Daily activities, meetings, and rooms can be scheduled. Each user has a personal calendar and can choose to have the computer remind him or her of a scheduled activity. Group scheduling of user calendars allows one user to schedule meetings and appointments without endless phone calls. The calendar can also be used to start application programs at specific dates and times.

REVIEW QUESTIONS

1. Why would a company need to purchase a midrange, multi-user computer system?

2. What are the security advantages of the IBM AS/400 over a typical system?

3. Define Control Language.

4. Define subsystem.

5. What is an object on the AS/400?

6. What are the six major functions of PC Support?

7. Define physical file.

8. Define logical file.

EXERCISES

1. The AS/400 comes with many manuals. Does your installation have the paper manuals or manual images on a CD-ROM? Do you have access to these manuals?

   If you do have access to these manuals, locate the Master Index manual. What is its purpose?

   Your instructor may give you additional exercises to learn how to use the manuals.

2. What level of security is your AS/400 running under?

3. What model of the AS/400 are you working on? How much memory and storage space does it have?

4. What programming languages does your AS/400 support?

Hands-On the AS/400

To learn how to sign on and off the AS/400.

To utilize the online tutorials.

SIGNING ON THE AS/400

Before you can sign on and use the AS/400, the Security Officer must have created a user profile just for you. This user profile specifies your userid and password, how much space you are allowed, what your priority will be, and what type of job you will be performing. For example, an operator will be allowed access to different commands than a programmer.

Your instructor will provide you with your userid and password. Both of these must be entered on the **Sign On** screen to allow access to the AS/400. If the screen is blank and the power is on, touch any key to display the **Sign On** screen or turn up the brightness. Refer to the proper display station manual for information on its operation. See Figure 2.1 for the **Sign On** screen.

```
                              Sign On
                                      System  . . . . . :   XXXXXXX
                                      Subsystem . . . . :   XXXXX
                                      Display . . . . . :   XXXXXXXX

              User  . . . . . . . . . . . . .    _____
              Password  . . . . . . . . . . .
              Program/procedure . . . . . . .    _____
              Menu  . . . . . . . . . . . . .    _____
              Current library . . . . . . . .    _____












                                      (C) COPYRIGHT IBM CORP. 1980, 1991.
```

FIGURE 2.1   Sign On Screen

The **Sign On** screen gives you three facts about the AS/400 on which you will be working. The System number is the IBM serial number or installation name of this particular AS/400. The Subsystem name is the named area in main storage where your jobs will be run. The Display is the system's name of the display station on which you are working. These values will vary as you change systems.

The userid will normally be your first initial and up to six characters of your last name. If your name is less than the maximum, you do not need to type in spaces. Simply enter your userid and press the Field Exit key. The next item on the **Sign On** screen is the password. Your instructor will assign your initial password. The Program/procedure, Menu, and Current Library values may be entered to take you directly to a given task. For this text, these will remain blank.

Type	`userid`	on the User line
Press	`Field Exit`	to go to the next line
Type	`your password`	for the password
Press	`Enter`	to bypass the remaining options

PASSWORDS

If this is the first time you are signing on to the system, you might be instructed to change your password. This option is set by the Security Officer, and the password might not be mandated to change. See Figure 2.2 for the **Password Expired** screen.

```
                      Sign-on Information
                                              System:    XXXXXXXX
Password has expired. Password must be changed to continue sign-on
request.




        Press F9 to change your password.

        F3=Exit sign-on request  F9=Change password
        (C) COPYRIGHT IBM CORP. 1980, 1991.
```

FIGURE 2.2   Password Expired Screen

Press	`F9`	to change your password

A password has one to ten characters but can be predetermined by your Security Officer. See Figure 2.3 for the **Change Password** screen. The first character must be a letter (A–Z), and the remaining characters can be any letter or number but may not contain spaces. It is a good habit to have a password that is three to six characters. The password is invisible as you type it in. The longer the password, the easier it is to make a typing error.

```
                          Change Password

Password last changed . . . . . . . . . . :    02/02/92

Type choices, press Enter.

  Current password  . . . . . . . . . . .

  New password  . . . . . . . . . . . . .

  New password (to verify)  . . . . . . .








  F3=Exit           F12=Cancel
```

FIGURE 2.3   *Change Password Screen*

No one has access to your password but you. Your password cannot be accessed by anyone but you, so do not forget it. Do not make the password something that your friends will be able to easily guess. If you forget your password, the Security Officer can reset your password to your userid.

Type	current password	
Press	Field Exit	
Type	new password	
Press	Field Exit	
Type	new password	type it again
Press	Enter	

When you sign on the next time, you will need to use the new password.

MAIN MENU

See Figure 2.4 for the **AS/400 Main Menu**. This is the starting point for accessing everything on the AS/400. From this menu, you can access many other menus and options in the system. Take a moment to look at the selections that are available.

The cursor is a flashing underline and should currently be located at the beginning of the command line. The command line is under the words "Selection or command" and to the right of the arrow, ⇒. You can use the cursor movement keys to move around the screen. However, the only place you can enter a menu selection or command is on the command line. If you want more information about any menu selection, move the cursor to that selection and press the Help key.

```
MAIN                          AS/400 Main Menu
                                                    System:   XXXXXXXX
 Select one of the following:

       1. User tasks
       2. Office tasks
       3. General system tasks
       4. Files, libraries, and folders
       5. Programming
       6. Communications
       7. Define or change the system
       8. Problem handling
       9. Display a menu
      10. User support and education
      11. PC Support tasks

      90. Sign off

 Selection or command
 ===>_____


 F3=Exit   F4=Prompt   F9=Retrieve   F12=Cancel   F13=User support
 F23=Set initial menu
 (C) COPYRIGHT IBM CORP. 1980, 1991.
```

FIGURE 2.4   AS/400 Main Menu

WORKING WITH FUNCTION KEYS

Notice the function keys that apply to this menu listed on the *bottom of the screen.* The function keys refer to the two rows of keys at the top of the keyboard, all of which have an "F" before the key number. Most AS/400 screen displays will list the active keys at the bottom of the screen. Any function key that is not listed on the screen will not be understood by the system. Depending on the function of the screen, the active keys are different. If you see "F24=More keys," there are more keys active than the screen has room for. If you then press F24, you see additional function keys and their actions displayed. You might need to press F24 more than once to see all of the available function keys. F24 works as a toggle key, and when it is pressed again (or again), the original selection of function keys is displayed.

If you see "F5=Refresh", your screen will be updated with current values by pressing F5. On some screens, the data may be changed by you or the system after it initially appears on the display station. To see the new values, you will need to refresh the screen. The original screen remains unless you refresh the screen or exit and return.

ONLINE TUTORIALS

The AS/400 comes with an extensive set of online tutorials. These tutorials may be completed in their entirety, or you may ask the system to select modules for your particular needs. The AS/400 has a set of tutorials for a user, a manager, a programmer, and other audience paths.

To begin the online tutorials, you should be at the **Main Menu**. See Figure 2.4 for the **Main Menu** screen.

Type	10	on the command line
Press	Enter	

See Figure 2.5 for the **User Support and Education** menu.

```
 SUPPORT                    User Support and Education
                                                      System:   XXXXXXXX
 Select one of the following:

          1. How to use help
          2. Search system help index
          3. How to use commands
          4. Question and answer
          5. AS/400 publications
          6. IBM product information
          7. How to handle system problems
          8. Problem handling
          9. Online education




 Selection or command
 --->_____
 _____
 F3=Exit   F4=Prompt   F9=Retrieve   F12=Cancel   F16=AS/400 main menu
 (C) COPYRIGHT IBM CORP. 1980, 1991.
```

FIGURE 2.5   *User Support and Education Menu*

Type	9	for Online Education
Press	Enter	

See Figure 2.6 for registering for the online education tutorials.

The AS/400 will track your progress and will mark each unit complete as you finish the module.

Type	your first name
Press	Field Exit
Type	your last name
Press	Enter

The **Select Course** menu is displayed in Figure 2.7

```
                          Specify Your Name

   To begin online education, type name and press Enter.

      Student:
        First name . . . . . . . .  _____
        Last name  . . . . . . . .  _____
```
```
   F3=Exit    F12=Cancel
```

FIGURE 2.6   Registering for Online Education

```
                          Select Course
   Type option, press Enter.
     1=Select    8=Display description

   Option      Course Title
     _         Tutorial System Support (TSS)
```
```
                                                        Bottom
   F3=Exit    F9=Print list    F12=Cancel    F17=Top    F18=Bottom
```

FIGURE 2.7   Select Course Menu

Select the Tutorial System Support by typing a 1 in the option column. Or you may display the description of the tutorial with an 8 in the option column.

Type	1	in the option column for tutorial system support
Press	Enter	

As shown in Figure 2.8, the **Select Audience Path** menu allows you to select a subset of the available tutorials based on your job or interest.

```
                        Select Audience Path

   Course title . . . . . . . . :   Tutorial System Support (TSS)

   Type option, press Enter.
     1=Select    5=Display modules    8=Display description

   Option      Audience Path Title
     _          How to Use AS/400 Online Education
     _          All Modules in the Course
     _          Communications Implementer
     _          Database Administrator
     _          Data Processing Manager
     _          Executives
     _          Office Systems Administrator
     _          Clerical User (Secretary)
     _          Office Implementer
     _          Experienced S/36 System Operator
     _          Experienced S/38 System Operator
     _          Programmer/Implementer
     _          Professional User
                                                            More...
   F3=Exit    F9=Print list    F12=Cancel    F17=Top    F18=Bottom
```

FIGURE 2.8   Select Audience Path Menu

Figure 2.8 displays the online tutorial modules that are of interest to different people. For example, a user would need less information than a programmer would require. For this text, you will use the Work Station Operator audience path. You can choose another audience path at any time if you want to view other modules.

Select the work station operator path.

Press	Shift/Up Arrow

See Figure 2.9 for the second page of audience path titles.

Type	1	in the option column for Work Station Operator
Press	Enter	

See Figure 2.10 for the **Select Course Option** menu.

```
                          Select Audience Path

  Course title . . . . . . . . :  Tutorial System Support (TSS)

  Type option, press Enter.
    1=Select    5=Display modules    8=Display description

  Option      Audience Path Title
    _         Experienced S/36 Programmer/Implementer
    _         Experienced S/38 Programmer/Implementer
    _         System Analyst
    _         System Operator
    _         Work Station Operator




                                                         Bottom

  F3=Exit    F9=Print list   F12=Cancel   F17=Top   F18=Bottom
```

FIGURE 2.9   *Select Audience Path Menu, page 2*

```
                        Select Course Option

  Course title . . . . . . . . :  Tutorial System Support (TSS)
  Audience path title . . . . :  Work Station Operator
  Next module  . . . . . . . :  Getting Started with Online Education
  Bookmark module . . . . . . :

  Select one of the following:

    Education Options
        1. Start next module

        3. Select module in audience path

    Change Enrollment
        4. Select audience path
        5. Select course


  Selection _


  F3=Exit    F12=Cancel
```

FIGURE 2.10   *Select Course Option Menu*

Option 1 gives you every module in the Work Station Operator path, one after another. Option 3 allows you to select from the 13 tutorial modules in the Work Station Operator audience path. At this time you need to select only certain modules.

Type	3	in the Selection blank
Press	Enter	

See Figure 2.11 for a list of some of the tutorial modules available on the AS/400. You will not need to view all of these modules at this time. The modules that you will need to view are listed at the end of the chapter in the exercises. These selected modules will explain the concepts of how the AS/400 functions and will enhance your performance when you are using the machine.

```
                    Select Module in Audience Path

   Course title . . . . . . . . :    Tutorial System Support (TSS)
   Audience path title . . . . :    Work Station Operator

   Type option, press Enter.
     1=Select   8=Display description

   Option  Module Title                                 PC Req    Date
     _     Getting Started with Online Education         No
     _     An Additional Way to Select Modules           No
     _     Additional Functions in Online Education      No
     _     Computer Fundamentals- System Components      No
     _     Computer Fundamentals- Handling Data          No
     _     Computer Fundamentals- Programming            No
     _     Introduction to Operating Systems             No
     _     How to Use AS/400 Menus                       No
     _     Working with System Displays                  No
     _     How to Use AS/400 Help Support                No
     _     How to Send, View, and Respond to Messages    No
     _     Displaying and Controlling Printed Output     No
                                                               More...

   F3=Exit   F9=Print list   F12=Cancel   F17=Top   F18=Bottom
```

FIGURE 2.11   *Available AS/400 Tutorial Modules*

SIGNING OFF THE COMPUTER

When you have completed your work on the AS/400, you *must* sign off the system. If you do not sign off, the next user could access your work, delete your reports, and exhaust all your assigned resources. There are two methods for signing off.

Press	F3	repeatedly to return to the Main Menu
Type	90	Option 90 on the Main Menu is to sign off
Press	Enter	

OR

Type	signoff	on any command line
Press	Enter	

1. Explain the use of the function keys F5 and F24.

2. Why should you use the Signoff command or option 90 (Sign off) on the **Main Menu**?

3. Describe the purpose of the **User Support and Education** menu.

4. Define the purpose of an audience path. Explain how it can help you. How is the audience path modified?

Complete these tutorials before you go any further in this text. Answer the questions below as you are reading through the tutorials. To select a module, type a 1 in the option column and press Enter. Each tutorial takes approximately 30 minutes to complete.

> Getting Started with Online Education
> How to Use AS/400 Menus
> How to Use AS/400 Help Support
> Optional: Introduction to Operating Systems
> Optional: Computer Fundamentals—Programming

1. *Getting Started with Online Education* is the first tutorial to be read. Answer the following questions as you are reading.

   a. How do you access the **Select Student Option** menu?
   b. How many hints are there to any question in a module?
   c. How do you find the solution to a question?
   d. How do you return to a previous menu? Why would you want to do this?

2. *How to Use AS/400 Menus* is the second tutorial to be read. Answer the following questions as you are reading.

   a. What other key performs the same function as Help (Scroll Lock on a PC)?
   b. Explain the concept of menu chaining.
   c. How do you implement the "fast path" method to request a menu?

3. *How to Use AS/400 Help Support* is the third tutorial to be read. Answer the following questions as you are reading.

   a. What key brings up the **User Support and Education** menu?
   b. How do you initiate Field Help?
   c. What is the purpose of the Search Help Index?

4. An optional tutorial is *Introduction to Operating Systems*. Read this if you would like more information on the OS/400 operating system.

5. Another optional tutorial is *Computer Fundamentals—Programming*. Read this if you would like more information on programming.

6. Access any of the other tutorials in your audience path as time permits. These tutorials are excellent references when you are having difficulties in learning the AS/400.

The following exercises will allow you to "walk around" the AS/400. Remember that the F3 key will return you to a menu, while the F12 key takes you back to the previous screen, whether it is a menu or another type of display.

If you are still signed on the system, sign off.

7. Sign on to the AS/400 using your new password.

8. From the **Main Menu,** select the **User Tasks** menu. How many options are available on this menu? Select option 5, Programming. How many options are there on the **Programming** menu? Return to the **Main Menu.**

9. Select several other menus, and see what they do. Remember to use the Help key to learn more about the options. Record at least three options that you selected and what you learned about the AS/400.

10. List two rules for creating valid passwords.

11. What action should you take when you see "More..." at the lower right-hand corner of a screen?

Messages

To understand the AS/400 system message function.

To learn how to send and receive messages.

INTRODUCTION

The AS/400 uses messages as its method of communication between you and the computer or between you and another user. Messages can be sent by the system to a user, or messages can be sent within the system from program to program, or messages can be sent from one user to another user.

There are two basic types of messages on the AS/400: informational and inquiry. An informational message could be a notification that a job has been completed or that the system operator needs all users to sign off. These messages do not require a response from the user. Inquiry messages give information and expect a response from the user. A system inquiry message usually waits for a response before continuing with its processing. A user could utilize an inquiry message to ask for information, using the message queue as a form of electronic mail.

The way in which a user receives a message depends on the action that generated the message. Messages can be displayed in three ways: on the message line of a display screen (the bottom line), on a break message display screen, or on a user-requested display message screen.

Messages that appear on a message line are normally in response to a request to the system. These can be messages explaining that an event or an error has occurred.

System and user messages can also be break messages. Break messages appear directly on the display and have priority over the work being done. Whenever a break message is received, the current display is saved, and work can be resumed when the message has been reviewed and/or answered.

Some system messages and most user messages are sent to a user's message queue. Remember that a message queue is a mailbox for messages. When a message is placed into the message queue, the user is notified by a buzzer and/or a message waiting light on the display screen. A display station will show a "torn corner" symbol in the lower left of the indicator line, while a PC will have the "MW" highlighted on the indicator line.

SYSTEM MESSAGES

There are many predefined system messages. When a source member is compiled, the user receives a system message that a compile batch job has been started. If a program aborts during execution, a system break message is sent to the user. If a file has been sent to a printer and the printer is not turned on, a message will be sent to the system operator and to the user who requested the print job to turn on the printer.

The AS/400 sends informational or inquiry messages depending on the system event. A user often receives a system message in response to a command that has been entered on the command line. These system messages usually appear at the bottom of the current display, below the function key area. In Figure 3.1, the F5 function key was pressed in error.

```
MAIN                        AS/400 Main Menu
                                                     System:   XXXXXXXX
 Select one of the following:

      1. User tasks
      2. Office tasks
      3. General system tasks
      4. Files, libraries, and folders
      5. Programming
      6. Communications
      7. Define or change the system
      8. Problem handling
      9. Display a menu
     10. User support and education
     11. PC Support tasks

     90. Sign off

 Selection or command
 ==>_____


 F3=Exit   F4=Prompt   F9=Retrieve   F12=Cancel   F13=User support
 F23=Set initial menu
 Function key not allowed
```

FIGURE 3.1   *System Message as Result of Accidentally Pressing F5*

If a plus sign (+) is shown at the far right of the message line, the message will not fit on one line. Position the cursor on the message and press Shift/Roll Up to display the remainder of the message information. Pressing the Help key with the cursor on the message will also give additional message information.

When a system message is a break message, it is normally an inquiry message and requires a response. A typical system break message is that a program cannot proceed because of a run time error and needs to be canceled. But before the system cancels the program, the AS/400 asks whether the user wants a system dump. Inquiry messages list the accepted response options. Placing the cursor on the message and pressing the Help key gives more information about the message and its options. Figure 3.2 is an example of an RPG program run time error.

By moving the cursor to the actual message and pressing the Help key, the **Additional Message Information** screen shown in Figure 3.3 will be seen.

Figure 3.3 shows additional information that explains the meaning of the acceptable responses and directs the programmer to the line in the RPG source member that is causing the error.

```
                        Display Program Messages


Job xxxxxxx/userid/xxxxx started on 11/19/91 at 08:18:07 in subsystem XXXXXXXX
1600 decimal-data error in field (C G S D F).

















Type reply, press Enter.
  Reply . . . _____
       _____

F3=Exit    F12=Cancel
```

FIGURE 3.2   Display Program Messages

```
                      Additional Message Information

Message ID . . . . . . : RPG0907          Severity . . . . :  99
Message type . . . . . : INQUIRY
Date sent  . . . . . . : 11/19/91          Time sent. . . . :  08:18
From program . . . . . : QRGXMSG           Instruction. . . :  0000
To program . . . . . . : *EXT              Instruction. . . :  0000

Message. . :  RPG101 1600 decimal-data error in field (C G S D F).
Cause. . . :  The RPG program RPG101 in library userid found a decimal-data
  error at statement 1600.  One field did not contain valid numeric data.  The
  digit and/or sign is not valid.
Recovery . :  Enter C to cancel, G to continue processing at *GETIN, S to obtain
  a system dump, or D to obtain an RPG formatted dump.
Possible choices for replying to message . . . . . . . . . . :
  D -- Obtain RPG formatted dump.
  S -- Obtain system dump.
  G -- Continue processing at *GETIN.
  C -- Cancel.
  F -- Obtain full formatted dump.
Press Enter to continue.

F3=Exit          F10=Display messages in job log          F12=Cancel
```

FIGURE 3.3   Additional Message Information

| SENDING | Messages can be sent to anyone on the system if that person's userid is known. You can |
| MESSAGES | even send messages to yourself. Now send an informational message. |

Type	SNDMSG	on any command line
Press	F4	the Prompt key

Figure 3.4 shows the **Send Message** screen.

```
                          Send Message (SNDMSG)

 Type choices, press Enter.

 Message text . . . . . . . . . . _____
 _____
 _____
 _____
 _____
 _____
 _____

 To user profile  . . . . . . . .   _____  Name, *SYSOPR, *ALLACT...




                                                                   Bottom
 F3=Exit    F4=Prompt    F5=Refresh    F10=Additional parameters  F12=Cancel
 F13=How to use this display          F24=More keys
```

FIGURE 3.4   Send Message Command Screen

Type the message you want to send, using word wrap. Do not press the Tab key, the arrow keys, or the Enter key at the end of a line. Allow the operating system to determine when a line is full. The default message type is informational. Press Field Exit to move to the User profile name. Type a classmate's userid, or enter your own userid if you do not wish to disturb your neighbor.

Type	the message	ignore full lines
Press	Field Exit	when the message is finished
Type	the userid	of the message receiver
Press	Enter	

If an invalid userid is entered, a system message will be displayed, stating that the user profile was not found and that the message was not sent. However, if the message was sent successfully, no message is generated.

To receive a response to a message, an inquiry message must be sent. Notice the F10=Additional Parameters key.

Type	SNDMSG	on any command line
Press	F4	the Prompt key
Press	F10	for additional parameters

Figure 3.5 shows the additional parameters.

```
                        Send Message (SNDMSG)

 Type choices, press Enter.

 Message text . . . . . . . . . . _____
 _____
 _____
 _____
 _____
 _____
 _____

 To user profile  . . . . . . .   _____  Name, *SYSOPR, *ALLACT...

                       Additional Parameters

 To message queue . . . . . . .    _____    Name, *SYSOPR
    Library  . . . . . . . . . .   *LIBL        Name, *LIBL, *CURLIB
                 + for more values
                                   *LIBL
 Message type . . . . . . . . .    *INFO       *INFO, *INQ
                                                             More...
 F3=Exit   F4=Prompt   F5=Refresh   F12=Cancel   F13=How to use this display
 F24=More keys
```

FIGURE 3.5   Additional Send Message Parameters

The system attempts to reduce the amount of typing required to key any given command. The AS/400 assumes the most likely response and enters this as the default value for a parameter. There is a standard convention for displaying default values and then listing either all of the possible choices or at least the most commonly used options. This convention is displayed on the **Send Message** screen. Currently, the default message type is informational (*INFO). Changing the message type to *INQ, for inquiry, will require the receiver to respond to the message.

Type	a message	
Press	Field Exit	
Type	a userid	
Press	Field Exit	
Press	Tab	to move to the message type
Type	*INQ	to change the message type
Press	Shift/Roll Up	to move to the next page

```
                          Send Message (SNDMSG)

Type choices, press Enter.

Message queue to get reply . . .    *WRKSTN      Name, *WRKSTN
  Library . . . . . . . . . .       _____   Name, *LIBL, *CURLIB

















                                                                Bottom
F3=Exit   F4=Prompt   F5=Refresh   F12=Cancel   F13=How to use this display
F24=More keys
```

FIGURE 3.6   Send Message Command Screen, page 2

Figure 3.6 shows that the message queue that receives the reply defaults to the workstation. Remember that a workstation is a physical device and that you may move to a different workstation. Therefore the default must be changed to be the userid receiving the message. Because you want the reply to come to your userid, you must enter your userid here.

Type	your userid	to change the message queue to place the reply in your message queue
Press	Enter	

MESSAGE QUEUE

Most messages go to a user's message queue. A user profile is normally set up to receive messages in notify mode. Therefore when a message is placed into the queue, a user is notified by a buzzer and/or a message waiting light on the display screen.

View the messages in your message queue.

Type	DSPMSG	or **WRKMSG** on any command line
Press	Enter	

See Figure 3.7 for the **Work with Messages** screen.

If you had any messages at this time, each message would be listed individually.

```
                              Work with Messages
                                                    System:    XXXXXXXX
           Messages for:    YOURNAME

           Type options below, then press Enter.
             4=Remove    5=Display details and reply

           Opt    Message
                                    Messages needing a reply
                 (No messages available)

                                    Messages not needing a reply
                 (No messages available)




                                                                   Bottom
           F1=Help    F3=Exit    F5=Refresh    F6=Display system operator messages
           F16=Remove messages not needing a reply    F17=Top    F24=More keys
```

FIGURE 3.7   Work with Messages Screen

RESPOND TO AN INQUIRY MESSAGE

Type	5	in the option column
Press	Enter	

A screen will be shown for you to reply to the message. The reply is automatically sent back to the user who sent the inquiry message. The message is placed in that user's message queue or in the workstation message queue if the default value was not changed.

When a message is deleted, you will receive a confirmation request. This confirmation is to verify the delete. You must press Enter again to actually delete the message.

Type	4	in the option column
Press	Enter	
Press	Enter	again to confirm the delete

REVIEW QUESTIONS

1. Explain the difference between informational and inquiry messages.
2. What type(s) of messages does the operating system send?
3. What type(s) of messages can a user send?
4. Describe the ways in which messages can be received.
5. What CL command is used to send a message?
6. What two CL commands are used to view your messages?

EXERCISES

1. Send an informational message to yourself, a classmate, *and* your instructor.

2. Send an inquiry message to yourself, a classmate, and your instructor. Be sure to follow up on these messages; send additional messages to your classmate and instructor if they have not responded within several days.

3. Display your message queue. Do you have any messages?

4. For additional information on messages, review the online tutorial *How to Send, View, and Respond to Messages.* Also, there is more information in the AS/400 manual, New User's Guide.

Objects and Programming Development Manager (PDM)

To understand the concepts of libraries, objects, and members.

To understand how to work with PDM.

AS/400 OBJECTS

Objects and Libraries
—

Anything that exists and occupies space on an AS/400 disk is an object. There are many types of objects: data files, file descriptions, machine executable code, and so on. Objects that you create and work with on the AS/400 are created in a library. An AS/400 library is also an object and is an area on disk where related objects are stored. Each student in an AS/400 class will have a library, just as in industry each programmer would have a library and each production job would belong to a library. A user can have more than one personal library, and a user also has access to system libraries.

Objects in a library are compared to rooms in a house in the following examples. An AS/400 disk stores many libraries. A house can have many rooms. Each room has a specific function, just as each library has a specific function. Different libraries can contain objects with the same name. Several of the libraries could contain a data file object named paydata. A test library could contain a test version of paydata, and there could be production libraries for weekly, biweekly, and monthly payroll files named paydata.

Each room in the house could contain a telephone, just as each library contains a paydata. Each paydata is unique, just as each telephone is unique. To talk on a particular phone, you have to know what room it is in. To access a particular paydata, you must know what library it is in. See Figure 4.1.

FIGURE 4.1   *Objects Within Libraries*

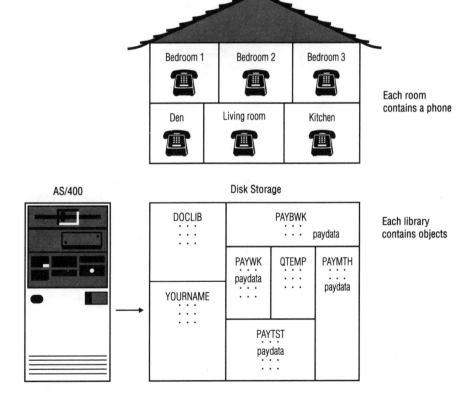

Object Type
———

The AS/400 must know what the object type is before any action can be performed on that object. The object is categorized with a type, which defines the object's characteristics. An object's type describes the content of the object. For example, an object can be data records, source records, machine-executable code, or an output queue.

All object types begin with an asterisk (*). Any object with a type of *FILE is similar to a file cabinet that contains other objects. The objects within a *FILE are called members because each member conforms to the characteristics of the file.

An object with a type of *PGM is machine-executable code. Objects of type *PGM do not contain members.

An object with a type of *OUTQ is an output queue, where print files are stored until printed or deleted.

Using the house example, a kitchen can contain many types of objects, including a cake and the cake recipe in a recipe box. The recipe is a list of instructions to make the cake. You can eat the results of the recipe, the cake, but you do not eat the recipe. See Figure 4.2.

FIGURE 4.2   ***Different Types of Objects Within a Library***

Kitchen

Objects in the Kitchen

Cake
Recipe box
Table
Chairs
Flowers in vase

Library (YOURNAME)

Program 2	Program 3		Source
	Program 1	File 2	
		File 1	
OUTQ			

Objects in YOURNAME

*FILE named SOURCE
*PGM named Program 1
*PGM named Program 2
*PGM named Program 3
*FILE named FILE1
*FILE named FILE2
*OUTQ named OUTQ

Object Attributes
———

Attributes further define the object. There are many attributes. For a complete list, see the AS/400 reference manuals. An object with a type of *FILE could have an attribute of:

PF-SRC	source physical file
PF-DTA	physical file data
LF	logical file

An object with a type of machine-executable code, *PGM, would have an attribute of the programming language source code:

CBL	for COBOL
CLP	for Control Language Program
RPG	for RPG/400

An object with a type of *OUTQ has no attributes.

Members
———

An object with a type of *FILE that has an attribute of PF-SRC (physical file–source) will contain only source code members. Program instruction source code and data description specifications for physical and logical files would be valid entries in a file object with an attribute of PF-SRC.

An object with a type of *FILE that has an attribute of PF-DTA (physical file–data) is a physical file. A physical file is an object that usually contains data. The records in the file are termed members. A physical file can have no members (termed an empty file) or many members. In this text, a physical file will contain only one member.

You may have three objects in your own student library that have been set up for you by your instructor. Two of the objects have your userid as the name of the object. Their types are *OUTQ, for your spooled output queue, and *JOBD, for your job description. The third object is a *FILE type, named SOURCE, which has an attribute of PF-SRC. SOURCE will contain any source file members that you create: RPG source code, COBOL source code, Control Language source code, and data description specifications for physical and logical files.

Source code members can be compared to the recipes in the recipe box. A recipe box can contain instructions for soup, bread, cake, cookies, and so on. A source physical file can contain members that are COBOL source code, RPG source code, and data description specifications for a physical file. See Figure 4.3 for clarification of members.

As an alternative to one source physical file, your class may be using separate source physical files for each type of source code member that you will be creating. Standard IBM naming conventions for source physical files include:

QCLSRC	CL source code
QCBLSRC	COBOL source code
QRPGSRC	RPG source code
QDDSSRC	Data Definition Specifications

FIGURE 4.3   *Members Within an Object*

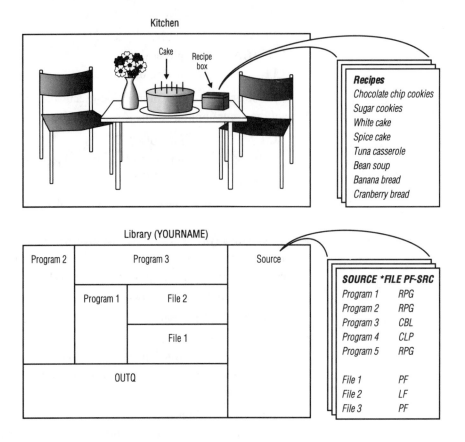

Library List

The authors of this text assume that you will be working in a library that has the same name as your userid. The userid library will become both your user library and the current library. The current library is defined in your user profile, and the authors assume that this is your userid library.

Each user has a library list that determines which libraries are searched and in what sequence the search is conducted. If you do not specify a library name when accessing an object, the system searches for the object in all of the libraries contained in your library list. Your library list has four parts: system libraries, licensed program libraries, the current library, and your user libraries. The system and licensed program libraries would normally be the same for all programming users.

A user can have as many user libraries as needed. You might have a user library named TEACHER, or some other name, that contains data files that the entire class can use. By having the TEACHER library in your library list, you will have easy access to your instructor's data files for any programming course.

The library list can be modified for each job that is run on the AS/400. As a student working in an interactive environment, your library list will probably remain stable. When the AS/400 expects to search the entire library list for an object, you will see the library name *LIBL (library list). If only the current library will be searched, you will see the library name *CURLIB. Libraries can be added to and removed from a library list temporarily or permanently, depending on the requirements of the job.

Searching a library list is similar to searching your house for your sunglasses. You know that they are in the house, so you begin a thorough room-by-room (or library-by-library) search. See Figure 4.4 for clarification of library lists.

FIGURE 4.4   ***Library List Search***

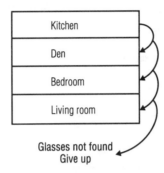

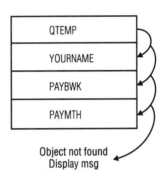

PROGRAMMING DEVELOPMENT MANAGER

Introduction to the Programming Development Manager

You will be using the Programming Development Manager (PDM) to work with the objects in your library. PDM is an AS/400 tool that allows access to other programming tools such as the Source Entry Utility (SEU) and the Data File Utility (DFU). PDM also allows access to print queues and message queues.

After you sign on to the AS/400, you will be at the **Main Menu**.

Type	5	on the command line to select Programming from the **Main Menu**
Press	Enter	

The **Programming** menu is displayed in Figure 4.5.

Working with the Programming Development Manager

To actually begin PDM,

Type	2	on the command line
Press	Enter	

See Figure 4.6.

You can type STRPDM and press Enter on the Main Menu command line to reach the PDM screen.

You are now in the Programming Development Manager, where you have access to your library, its objects, and any members within objects. Selection 1 will allow access to objects in a specific user library. If you have only one user library, you can

```
PROGRAM                        Programming
                                                    System:   XXXXXXXX
Select one of the following:

     1. Programmer menu
     2. Programming Development Manager (PDM)
     3. Utilities
     4. Programming language debug
     5. Structured Query Language (SQL) pre-compiler
     6. Question and answer
     7. IBM product information
     8. Copy screen image
     9. Cross System Product/Application Execution (CSP/AE)

    50. System/36 programming

    70. Related commands

Selection or command
==>_____

_____
F3=Exit   F4=Prompt   F9=Retrieve   F12=Cancel   F13=User support
F16=AS/400 Main menu
(C) COPYRIGHT IBM CORP. 1980, 1991.
```

FIGURE 4.5   Programming Menu

```
                    AS/400 Programming Development Manager (PDM)

Select one of the following:

     1. Work with libraries
     2. Work with objects
     3. Work with members

     9. Work with user-defined options







Selection or command
==>_____

_____
F3=Exit        F4=Prompt       F9=Retrieve      F10=Command entry
F12=Cancel     F18=Change defaults
                                    (C) COPYRIGHT IBM CORP. 1981, 1991.
```

FIGURE 4.6   Programming Development Manager Menu

use selection 2 to go to your objects, as the system uses the current user library as the default library. If you want to access members within an object, then choose selection 3.

Because you need to access objects stored within your library, you want the first selection to be "Work with libraries."

Type	1	on the command line
Press	Enter	

The **Specify Libraries to Work with** menu is shown in Figure 4.7.

```
                      Specify Libraries to Work with

  Type choice, press Enter.

     Library  . . . . . . . . . .   *LIBL       *LIBL, name, *generic*, *ALL,
                                                *ALLUSR, *USRLIBL, *CURLIB













  F3=Exit     F5=Refresh     F12=Cancel
```

FIGURE 4.7   Specifying Libraries to Work with

Type	your userid	as the library name if it does not appear on the library line

If you have already entered the library name in a previous AS/400 session, the operating system will use the default concept and provide this value for you.

Press	Enter

See Figure 4.8 for the **Work with Libraries Using PDM** screen.

There are many actions, using the options, available for your library. Options differ from functions keys in that options are always shown on the upper half of the screen. Options are for use with individual objects. Options are entered as numbers and can be keyed from the ten-key pad or from the top row of keys. The option number for the selected action is typed in the Opt column to the left of the desired object name. Depending on the *Type* of the object, you may be limited as to which options you can actually use.

```
                    Work with Libraries Using PDM

  List type  . . . . . . .   *ALL           Position to . . . . .

  Type options, press Enter.
    2=Change       3=Copy                    4=Delete      5=Display
    7=Rename       8=Display description     9=Save        10=Restore ...

  Opt  Library    Type     Text
   __  YOURNAME   *TEST    Your Name LIBRARY




                                                              Bottom
     Parameters or command
     ==>_____
     F3=Exit         F4=Prompt         F5=Refresh        F6=Create
     F9=Retrieve     F10=Command entry F23=More options  F24=More keys
```

FIGURE 4.8   Work with Libraries Using PDM

Options perform different operations on an object, including change, copy, delete, display, rename, and so on.

Press	F23	to see more options
Type	12	before your library in the option column to "work with" objects
Press	Enter	

The **Work with Objects Using PDM** screen is displayed in Figure 4.9.

To go directly to this screen, type WRKOBJPDM on any command line and press Enter.

As you begin this course, you may have three objects in your library. The SOURCE object (type *FILE, attribute PF-SRC) will contain all of the source code that you create. Your output queue (*OUTQ) will retain printed output for you to display on the screen and print if needed.

The job description (*JOBD), if present, is being used to supply an expanded library list to your interactive session, as well as to any batch jobs that you submit. Remember that a library can also contain machine-executable code and physical files with data.

There are many options for working with objects. Only certain options are available, depending on the type of the object. You will receive an error message if an option cannot be used with a given object. The options available on this **Work with Objects Using PDM** screen and a short definition of each are shown in Figure 4.10.

```
                    Work with Objects Using PDM

    Library . . . . .   YOURNAME        Position to . . . . . . . .
                                        Position to type  . . . . .

    Type options, press Enter.
      2=Change        3=Copy        4=Delete      5=Display      7=Rename
      8=Display description         9=Save       10=Restore     11=Move ...

    Opt  Object     Type       Attribute  Text
    __   YOURNAME   *OUTQ                  Your Name OUTQ
    __   SOURCE     *FILE      PF-SRC      Your Name SOURCE
    __   YOURNAME   *JOBD                  Your Name JOB DESC




                                                                    Bottom
    Parameters or command
    ==>_____
    F3=Exit         F4=Prompt           F5=Refresh        F6=Create
    F9=Retrieve     F10=Command entry   F23=More options  F24=More keys
```

FIGURE 4.9   Work with Objects Using PDM

FIGURE 4.10	**Work with Objects Using PDM Options**	
	2 = CHANGE	To change certain attributes of an object.
	3 = COPY	To duplicate an object in the same library or to copy an object to a different library.
	4 = DELETE	To delete an object in a library.
	5 = DISPLAY	To display more information about an object.
	7 = RENAME	To change the name of an object.
	8 = DISPLAY DESCRIPTION	To display a description of an object.
	9 = SAVE	To save an object on diskette or tape.
	10 = RESTORE	To restore an object from diskette or tape.
	11 = MOVE	To move an object from one library to another.
	12 = WORK WITH	To work with an object. This is used to work with members of *FILE objects when the attribute is PF-SRC or PF-DTA.
	13 = CHANGE TEXT	To change the text description of an object.
	15 = COPY FILE	To copy specific members or records of a member. This option has more flexibility than option 3.
	16 = RUN	To run, or execute, an object (for example a CL, COBOL, or RPG program).
	18 = CHANGE USING DFU	To use the Data File Utility to change a data physical file.
	25 = FIND STRING	To search data physical files or source physical files for a given character string.

Remember from the tutorial *How to Use AS/400 Help Support* that by placing the cursor on the option area of the screen you will receive more information about each option.

The function keys provide you with information about the display screen. The function keys do not help you with individual objects.

You will store all of the source code that you create as members within the source physical file object named SOURCE. These members can include physical and logical file descriptions, screen formats, and language source code (COBOL, RPG, CL, and so on). You will need to "Work with" your SOURCE object to access the individual members. Option 12 is used to access members within objects. Option 12 will be used with SOURCE and your output queue.

Type	12	next to the SOURCE object in the Opt (option) column
Press	Enter	

See Figure 4.11 for the **Work with Members Using PDM** screen.

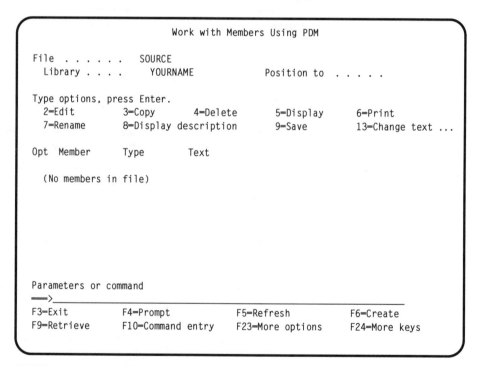

FIGURE 4.11   Work with Members Using PDM

You are now working *within* your SOURCE file. The file name and the library name are at the top of the screen. This **Work with Members Using PDM** screen is where source members will be created and edited. Notice that this screen has options for working with the members, similar to options on the last screen, **Work with Objects Using PDM**. These options are only for source members. A short description of each of these options is shown in Figure 4.12.

FIGURE 4.12	**Work with Members Using PDM Options**	

2 = Edit	To edit a member using the Source Entry Utility (SEU).
3 = Copy	To duplicate a member within SOURCE or to copy to another source file or library.
4 = Delete	To delete a member.
5 = Display	To display a member using SEU (to browse).
6 = Print	To print a member. The spooled file is place into your output queue with a QPSUPRTF file name.
7 = Rename	To change a member name.
8 = Display description	To display information about a member.
9 = Save	To save a member to diskette or tape.
13 = Change text	To change the text description of a member.
14 = Compile	To compile a member. The system creates an object based on the member being compiled. If the object already exists, the **Confirm Compile of Member** screen will appear.
16 = Run procedure	To run certain types of members.
17 = Change using SDA	To start the Screen Design Aid (SDA) utility to edit menu and screen design members.
19 = Change using RLU	To use the Report Layout Utility (RLU) to work with report members.
25 = Find string	To search for a given character string in the members.

Use the Help key to learn more about these member options. And as with the object screen options, not all options are valid with each member. You will receive an error message if an invalid option is requested.

The F6 function key is used on this screen to create a new member within SOURCE. You define a member name and its type and give a description of the new member. You are then transferred to the Source Entry Utility (SEU) to key in the new source member code.

The remaining function keys help you work with what is displayed on your screen. These function keys are not for help with your members.

PDM REVIEW

1. To initiate PDM, you must first sign on to the system.

2. At the **Main Menu**, choose option 5 to initiate the **Programming** menu. Press Enter.

3. Choose option 2, Programming Development Manager (PDM). Press Enter.

4. Choose "Work with Libraries" by typing 1. Press Enter.

   a. If your library name is not shown on the **Specify Libraries to Work with** screen, type your userid as the library name. Press Enter.

b. On the **Work with Libraries Using PDM** screen, type 12 in the option column before your library to work with your library. Press Enter. You will be at the **Work with Objects Using PDM** screen.

5. Or choose "Work with Objects" by typing 2. Press Enter.

    a. Your current library will be shown on the **Specify Objects to Work with** screen. Press Enter.

    b. You will be at the **Work with Objects Using PDM** screen.

T I P   Another method of starting PDM is to type STRPDM on any command line. The STRPDM command will immediately display the **Programming Development Manager (PDM)** menu.

T I P   You can also start PDM with the WRKOBJPDM command. This command will immediately display the **Work with Objects Using PDM** screen. Your current library will be the default library for accessing the objects.

T I P   You can also start PDM with the WRKMBRPDM command. This command will immediately display the **Work with Members Using PDM** screen. Your current library will be the default library

---

REVIEW QUESTIONS

1. Describe the relationship of objects and libraries.

2. Define object type and object attribute.

3. Which type of objects can have members?

4. Define library list.

5. What objects are in your library?

6. Define PDM.

7. What are the options used for on the **Work with Objects Using PDM** and **Work with Members Using PDM** screens? How do they differ from the function keys?

8. Describe two methods of accessing the **Work with Objects Using PDM** screen.

9. Describe two methods of accessing the **Work with Members Using PDM** screen.

EXERCISES

1. Access the **Work with Object Using PDM** screen. Display the description (option 8) of each of the objects in your library. List the first two items displayed for each object.

2. Change the text description (option 13) of your SOURCE object by deleting either your first or last name. Change the text description back to what it was originally.

3. For additional information on PDM, review the online tutorial *AS/400 Application Development Tools Overview*. You will need to change your audience path to Programmer/Implementer to view this tutorial on PDM.

 T I P   To reach the **Select Course Option** screen quickly, type STREDU on any command line.

Printing

To understand how to display output on the screen.

To understand how to print output on the printer using Work with Output Queue.

To understand how to print output on the printer using Work with Printer Output.

INTRODUCTION

The AS/400 will automatically place printable output from jobs into spooled files on an output queue. An output queue is a storage area for spooled print files. You should have an output queue object that has the same name as your userid. Print jobs are spooled so that they can be released to the printer at the time that is most convenient to either the operator or the user. This makes efficient use of printer hardware and employee productivity. For this course, you might need to print a copy of a display screen. This screen display is put into a spooled file on an output queue.

AS/400 programmers and users need to learn to work with the screen images of output as much as possible. Any spooled file can be displayed on the screen. Programming errors can often be noted without printing a report, just by viewing the screen output. This saves time and money.

There is usually only one printer serving many display stations, and lengthy reports can tie up the printer. If several users direct output to the printer at the same time, there is no problem; the printer will print one file at a time until all the reports have been printed. In a production environment, lengthy spooled print files and reports that need special forms are typically released to a printer on the evening shift.

ACCESSING SPOOLED FILES THROUGH PDM

You will be using the Programming Development Manager (PDM) to access your output queue. Access the **Work with Objects Using PDM** screen, shown in Figure 5.1.

Type	WRKOBJPDM	on any command line
Press	Enter	

```
                    Work with Objects Using PDM

    Library . . . . .   YOURNAME        Position to . . . . . . . .
                                        Position to type  . . . . .


    Type options, press Enter.
      2=Change      3=Copy         4=Delete      5=Display    7=Rename
      8=Display description        9=Save       10=Restore   11=Move ...


    Opt  Object      Type      Attribute    Text
    __   YOURNAME    *OUTQ                  Your Name OUTQ
    __   SOURCE      *FILE     PF-SRC       Your Name SOURCE
    __   YOURNAME    *JOBD                  Your Name JOB DESC




                                                                  Bottom
    Parameters or command
    ==>_____
    F3=Exit          F4=Prompt         F5=Refresh        F6=Create
    F9=Retrieve      F10=Command entry  F23=More options  F24=More keys
```

FIGURE 5.1   Work with Objects Using PDM

There is an object named yourname (your userid), which has a type of *OUTQ. All of your print files will automatically go to this output queue. To view the print files in your output queue, you must work with your output queue. The "Work with" option is 12.

Type	12	before the output queue
Press	Enter	

Figure 5.2 shows the **Work with Output Queue** screen.

```
                         Work with Output Queue

   Queue:   YOURNAME       Library:   YOURNAME        Status:   RLS

   Type options, press Enter.
     1=Send   2=Change   3=Hold   4=Delete   5=Display   6=Release   7=Messages
     8=Attributes        9=Work with printing status

   Opt  File        User        User Data   Sts   Pages   Copies  Form Type   Pty
     (No spooled output files)




                                                                      Bottom
   Parameters for options 1, 2, 3, or command
   ==>_____
   F3=Exit    F11=View 2    F12=Cancel    F22=Printers    F24=More keys
```

FIGURE 5.2   Work with Output Queue with No Files

Because you have never generated a printer report, you have no output files. When you do have output, a variety of information about each print file is available. The file name will reference a program printer file name or a job log file name from an AS/400 utility program. The information in the user column will match your userid, and the pages will detail the number of pages in the file. If you press F11, you will see more information about the file, including the date and time it was created.

Notice that you also have options to perform operations on each printer file, just as you have options to perform operations on other objects and members. For the options available on the **Work with Output Queue** screen and a short definition, see Figure 5.3.

FIGURE 5.3	***Work with Output Queue Options***

1 = SEND	To send the spooled file to another network.
2 = CHANGE	To change the attributes of the spooled file. This is used to change the actual printer name.
3 = HOLD	To hold the spooled file.
4 = DELETE	To delete the spooled file.
5 = DISPLAY	To display the data in the spooled file on the screen.
6 = RELEASE	To release a spooled file from a hold status.
7 = MESSAGE	To display messages related to the printing status of a spooled file.
8 = ATTRIBUTES	To display the attributes of the spooled file.
9 = WORK WITH PRINTING STATUS	To display the printing status of a spooled file.

The F22 key transfers you to the **Work with All Printers** screen so that you can check on the status of a printer. A printer might have a message waiting, the printer might be stopped, or the paper might need to be aligned. The remaining function keys are to help you work with information on the display screen.

CREATING A PRINT FILE

You will now create and work with a print file.

Press	Print key	to copy the **Work with Output Queue** screen to a printer report file

You should see the following message at the bottom of the screen. "Printer operation complete to the default printer device file." This action has locked the keyboard.

Press	Reset key	to unlock the keyboard
Press	F5	to refresh the screen

You will see a file named QSYSPRT listed, as shown in Figure 5.4.

When you select the display option, you will be able to see the same output that can be printed on paper.

Type	5	
Press	Enter	

See Figure 5.5 to verify your work.

```
                          Work with Output Queue

Queue:   YOURNAME      Library:   YOURNAME      Status:   RLS

Type options, press Enter.
  1=Send   2=Change   3=Hold   4=Delete   5=Display   6=Release   7=Messages
  8=Attributes        9=Work with printing status

Opt  File         User        User Data    Sts   Pages   Copies  Form Type   Pty
 __  QSYSPRT      YOURNAME                  RDY     1       1     *STD         5




                                                                      Bottom
Parameters for options 1, 2, 3, or command
==>_____
F3=Exit   F11=View 2   F12=Cancel   F22=Printers   F24=More keys
```

FIGURE 5.4   Work with Output Queue with One File

```
                          Display Spooled File
File . . . . . :  QSYSPRT                     Page/Line   1/6
Control . . . . .  _____                     Columns    1 - 78
Find . . . . . .  _____
*...+....1....+....2....+....3....+....4....+....5....+....6....+....7....+...
                        Print Key Output                              Page
   9999999 XXXXX 999999              XXXXXXXX          02/23/92   11:55
   Display Device . . . . .:   XXXXXXXXXX
   User . . . . . . . . . .:   YOURNAME
                        Work with Output Queue
Queue:   YOURNAME      Library:   YOURNAME      Status:   RLS
Type options, press Enter.
  1=Send   2=Change   3=Hold   4=Delete   5=Display   6=Release   7=Messages
  8=Attributes        9=Work with printing status
Opt  File         User        User Data  Sts   Pages   Copies  Form Type   Pt
  (No spooled output files)
                                                                      Bottom


Parameters for options 1, 2, 3 or command
==>_____
F3=Exit   F11=View 2   F12=Cancel   F22=Printers   F24=More keys
                                                                      Bottom
F3=Exit   F12=Cancel   F19=Left   F20=Right   F24=More keys
```

FIGURE 5.5   Display Spooled File of Print Key Output

DISPLAYING A SPOOLED FILE

You can use the Shift/Roll keys to scroll through the file if it is longer than one screen. If you press F24, more function keys will be displayed. The F19 and F20 keys are for printer reports that are wider than the screen. To see the material that is on the right edge of the report, use the F20 key. To return to the left edge of the report, use the F19 key.

The Control and Find fields at the top of the screen allow material to be located in an expedient fashion. The Control field commands are always measured from the current location of the cursor. To advance one line, type **+1** on the control field line and press Enter. To advance two lines, type **+2** on the control line and press Enter. Conversely, to go back three lines, type **−3** on the control line and press Enter. To advance one page, type **p+1** on the control field line and press Enter. To advance four pages, type **p+4** on the control line and press Enter. Conversely, to go back three pages, type **p−3** on the control line and press Enter. To display the last page of the file, type **b** for bottom and press Enter. To return to the first page of the file, type **t** for top and press Enter. For additional information, place the cursor on the Control field and press Help.

Find is similar to the Control field in that the cursor is quickly moved to any text location that you specify. If the text occurs multiple times in the document, the system will position the cursor at the first occurrence of the information. Position the cursor on the Find field, type **for options**, and press F16. The cursor will be moved to the "Parameter for options 1, 2, 3 or command" line. For additional information, place the cursor on the Find field and press Help.

You might find it convenient to use both the Control field and Find field together. Assume that the cursor is near the bottom of the file and you wish to find some text that is above the cursor location. You can type **t** (for top) on the Control field, press Field Exit, type the text, and press F16. The system will place the cursor at the top of the file and then find the appropriate text. See Figure 5.6 for the use of both fields.

When you are finished displaying a file's contents, return to the **Work with Output Queue** screen.

Press	F12	to exit the current screen and return to the Work with Output Queue screen

SENDING A FILE TO THE PRINTER

To actually print a file on paper, you must change one of the spooled file attributes.

Type	2	before QSYSPRT in the option column
Press	Enter	

See Figure 5.7 for the **Change Spooled File Attributes** screen.

```
                        Display Spooled File
File . . . . . :  QSYSPRT                      Page/Line   1/6
Control . . . . .  I_____                      Columns    1 - 78
Find . . . . . .   for options_____
*...+....1....+....2....+....3....+....4....+....5....+....6....+....7....+...
                        Print Key Output                            Page
    9999999 XXXXX 999999                 XXXXXXXX         02/23/92   11:55
    Display Device . . . . .:   XXXXXXXXXX
    User . . . . . . . . . .:   YOURNAME
                        Work with Output Queue
  Queue:  YOURNAME        Library:  YOURNAME          Status:  RLS
  Type options, press Enter.
    1=Send   2=Change   3=Hold   4=Delete   5=Display   6=Release   7=Messages
    8=Attributes        9=Work with printing status
  Opt  File        User        User Data  Sts  Pages  Copies Form Type  Pt
    (No spooled output files)
                                                                    Bottom


  Parameters for options 1, 2, 3 or command
  ==>_____
  F3=Exit   F11=View 2   F12=Cancel   F22=Printers   F24=More keys
                                                                    Bottom

  F3=Exit   F12=Cancel   F19=Left   F20=Right   F24=More keys
```

FIGURE 5.6   Display Spooled File with Control and Find Fields

```
              Change Spooled File Attributes (CHGSPLFA)

  Type choices, press Enter.

  Spooled file . . . . . . . . . > QSYSPRT        Name, *SELECT
  Job name . . . . . . . . . . . > XXXXXXXXX      Name, *
    User . . . . . . . . . . . . >   YOURNAME     Name
    Number . . . . . . . . . . . >   015087       000000-999999
  Spooled file number . . . . . >  38             1-9999, *ONLY, *LAST
  Printer . . . . . . . . . . .    *OUTQ          Name, *SAME, *OUTQ
  Print sequence . . . . . . . .   *SAME          *SAME, *NEXT
  Form type . . . . . . . . . .    *STD           Form type, *Same, *STD
  Copies . . . . . . . . . . . .   1              1-255, *SAME
  Restart printing . . . . . . .   *STRPAGE       Number, *SAME, *STRPAGE...

                        Additional Parameters

  Output queue . . . . . . . . .   YOURNAME       Name, *SAME, *DEV
    Library . . . . . . . . . .    YOURNAME       Name, *LIBL, *CURLIB

                                                                    Bottom
  F3=Exit   F4=Prompt   F5=Refresh   F10=Additional parameters   F12=Cancel
  F13=How to use this display       F24=More keys
```

FIGURE 5.7   Change Spooled File Attributes

The cursor is positioned at the Printer line item. You need to change the name of the Printer from *OUTQ to PRT01 (or the name of the local printer. Ask your instructor if the printer name has been defined to something other than PRT01). This will direct your output to the line printer.

Type	prt01	or the name of your printer
Press	Enter	

The file will be sent to the printer, and the report will start printing whenever the printer has completed its other jobs. You will also be returned to the previous **Work with Output Queue** screen.

Press	F5	to refresh the screen

Any file that has been printed will no longer be listed.

Retrieve		your output from the printer

DELETING PRINT FILES

Create another print file.

Press	Print key	to copy the screen to a printer report file
Press	Reset key	to unlock the keyboard
Press	F5	to refresh the screen

If you do not want to keep a spooled print file, it can be deleted from your output queue. You will be asked to confirm the delete of any spooled file by pressing Enter again. Delete the print file now.

Type	4	to request the delete
Press	Enter	
Press	Enter	again to confirm the delete
Press	F5	to refresh the screen

By refreshing the screen you should see the original screen with the message of "No spooled output files." It is important to remember that once you print or delete a file, it is no longer available.

WORKING WITH OUTPUT QUEUES REVIEW

1. On the **Work with Objects Using PDM** screen, type a 12 in the option column before your *OUTQ and press Enter.

2. Each output file will be displayed on a single line.

3. To display a file, type a 5 in the option column prior to the file you wish to have displayed on the screen.

4. To move a file to the printer, the printer attribute must be changed. Type a 2 in the option column next to the file to be printed. The **Change Spooled File Attributes** screen will be displayed. The cursor is already positioned on the Printer line.

Change the value to prt01 (or your installation printer name) and press Enter. Go and get your output from the printer.

5. To delete a file from your output queue, type a 4 in the option column next to the file you wish to delete. Press Enter to begin the deleting process. The AS/400 will ask you to confirm the delete, and you will be required to press Enter again.

WORKING WITH SPOOLED FILES

There is a different method to access spooled printed files. This method is usually faster to access and provides different information about each spooled file. In this section you will be working with spooled files on the **Work with Printer Output** screen. Each spooled file on this screen is listed with the name of the program that created it or as QSYSPRT if it is a copy of a display screen. If a program creates more than one printer output file, the **Work with Output Queue** screen is preferable because it lists the name of each print file in addition to the program that created it.

To create and work with a print file, the Print key will be used to copy a screen to a printer spooled file.

Press	Print key	to copy the screen

You should see the following message at the bottom of the screen: "Printer operation complete to the default printer device file." This action has locked the keyboard.

Press	Reset key	to unlock the keyboard

Repeat the above instructions so that you have at least two print files listed on your output queue.

To access the **Work with Printer Output** display, type SP in the option column on the **Work with Objects Using PDM** screen or the **Work with Members Using PDM** screen.

Type	sp	in any option column
Press	Enter	

 You can also type WRKSPLF (Work with Spooled Files) on any command line.

Figure 5.8 will appear on your screen.

Each print file will have the same name, QSYSPRT, but if you request the date and time function key (F11), you will notice that each file was created at a different time.

Press	F11	to display the date and time

Figure 5.9 is similar to the **Work With Objects Using PDM** screen. The options that you will use most often are Display (5), Delete (4), and Start printing (10).

```
                          Work with Printer Output
                                                    System:    XXXXXXXX
          User . . . . . :   YOURNAME

          Type options below, then press Enter.  To work with printers, press F22.
            2=Change    3=Hold   4=Delete    5=Display          6=Release   7=Message
            9=Work with printing status     10=Start printing   11=Restart printing

               Printer/
          Opt    Output      Status
               Not Assigned
          __     QSYSPRT     Not assigned to printer (use Opt 10)
          __     QSYSPRT     Not assigned to printer (use Opt 10)




                                                                      Bottom
          F1= Help      F3=Exit   F5=Refresh   F9=Command line   F11=Dates/pages/forms
          F12=Cancel    F21=Select assistance level    F22=Work with printers
```

FIGURE 5.8   *Work with Printer Output*

```
                          Work with Printer Output
                                                    System:    XXXXXXXX
          User . . . . . :   YOURNAME

          Type options below, then press Enter.  To work with printers, press F22.
            2=Change    3=Hold   4=Delete    5=Display          6=Release   7=Message
            9=Work with printing status     10=Start printing   11=Restart printing

               Printer/
          Opt    Output      Date      Time      Pages   Copies  Form type
               Not Assigned
          __     QSYSPRT    02/23/92  12:04:20      1       1    *STD
          __     QSYSPRT    02/23/92  12:04:47      1       1    *STD




                                                                      Bottom
          F1= Help      F3=Exit   F5=Refresh   F9=Command line   F11=Display statuses
          F12=Cancel    F21=Select assistance level    F22=Work with printers
```

FIGURE 5.9   *Work with Printer Output with Date and Time*

When a file is displayed (option 5) on the screen, use the Shift/Roll keys to scroll through the file if it is longer than one screen. When you are finished displaying a file's contents, the F12 key will return you to the previous screen.

When a file requires printing,

Type	10	in the option column prior to the output name
Press	Enter	

You are required to assign the output to a printer as shown in Figure 5.10.

```
                    Assign Output to a Printer

   Printer output . . :   QSYSPRT

This printer output is not assigned to a printer.
To print the output, type the printer name below and then press Enter.


   Printer  . . . . . . _____        Name, F4 for list












  F1=Help    F3=Exit    F12=Cancel
```

FIGURE 5.10   *Assign Output to a Printer*

The system requires that you enter the printer name.

Type	prt01	or the name of your printer
Press	Enter	

You will return to the **Work with Printer Output** screen, and a message at the bottom of the screen will state the printer name. See Figure 5.11.

There will be a new status following the file name, "*Attempting to start." Refresh the screen and change this status information to the current status of the print file.

Press	F5 key	to refresh the screen
Retrieve		your output from the printer

If the file has completed printing, the file name will no longer be on the screen. However, if the file name is still displayed, there may be a message that a certain page number is currently printing. Or the status may be that the file is waiting to print, as other reports are currently using the printer. Or the status may state that you have a printer message.

```
                          Work with Printer Output
                                                    System:    XXXXXXXX
          User . . . . . :   YOURNAME

          Type options below, then press Enter.  To work with printers, press F22.
            2=Change   3=Hold   4=Delete    5=Display        6=Release   7=Message
            9=Work with printing status    10=Start printing   11=Restart printing


                Printer/
          Opt   Output      Status
                Not Assigned
          __    QSYSPRT     *Attempting to start (use F5)
          __    QSYSPRT     Not assigned to printer (use Opt 10)








                                                                        Bottom
          F1= Help     F3=Exit    F5=Refresh   F9=Command line   F11=Dates/pages/forms
          F12=Cancel   F21=Select assistance level    F22=Work with printers
          Printer output QSYSPRT moved to printer PRT01.
```

FIGURE 5.11   Work with Printer Output Status Changes

If you do not want to keep a file, it can be deleted from your output queue. You will be asked to confirm the delete of any spooled file by pressing Enter again. Delete the other print file now.

Type	4	to request the delete
Press	Enter	
Press	Enter	again to confirm the delete
Press	F5	to refresh the screen

By refreshing the screen you should see the original screen with the message of "No spooled output files."

Remember, once you print or delete a file, it is no longer available.

WORKING WITH PRINTER OUTPUT (SPOOLED FILES) REVIEW

1. Type **SP** in any option column on the **Work with Objects Using PDM** screen or the **Work with Members Using PDM** screen.

   Or

   Type **WRKSPLF** on any command line.

2. Each output file will be displayed on a single line.

3. To display a file, type a 5 in the option column prior to the file you wish to have displayed on the screen.

4. To move a file to the printer, type a 10 in the option column next to the file to be printed. The **Assign Output to a Printer** screen will be displayed. Type **prt01** (or

your installation printer name) and press Enter. Go and get your output from the printer.

5. To delete a file from your output queue, type a 4 in the option column next to the file you wish to delete. Press Enter to begin the deleting process. The AS/400 will ask you to confirm the delete, and you will be required to press Enter again.

REVIEW QUESTIONS

1. Name the two different screens on which you can see a list of your printer files.
2. How do you access the two different output file screens?
3. How do you determine the length of a print file before it is printed?
4. Define spooled file.

EXERCISES

Use the Print key to place print images of each of the following four screens into your output queue: **Main Menu**, **Programming** menu, **Work with Libraries Using PDM** screen, and **Work with Objects Using PDM** screen.

1. Beginning at the **Work with Objects Using PDM** screen, access your output queue with option 12, "Work with" command.
2. Display the **Main Menu**.
3. Delete this file.
4. Display and then print the **Programming** menu file.
5. Return to the **Work with Objects Using PDM** screen.
6. Access the **Work with Printer Output** screen.
7. Display the **Work with Libraries Using PDM** screen. Print this file.
8. Display the **Work with Objects Using PDM** screen and delete this file.
9. For additional information on printing, review the online tutorial *Displaying and Controlling Printed Output*.

To reach the **Select Course Option** screen quickly, type STREDU on any command line.

Creating a Physical File Description

To understand how to create a physical file member.

To learn how to use the SEU utility program.

To learn how to compile members.

INTRODUCTION TO DATA DESCRIPTION SPECIFICATIONS AND THE SOURCE ENTRY UTILITY

Traditionally, file descriptions can be found within each program. The field names vary from program to program, making program changes difficult. Field length and record length problems are common, thus leading to data inaccuracy and frustration.

Files on the AS/400 are normally described externally from the programs that use them. Externally described files provide a single source of data information, yielding data independence, data security, and data integrity. Programming is also easier, since the programmer knows that the data definition is not the cause of any program errors, as other programs are using the same record and field definitions.

In this chapter you will create an external physical file description for a data file. You will define the contents of each record, including field name, field length, and data type using Data Description Specifications (DDS). The physical file description source member must be keyed and compiled. A separate object of type PF-DTA will be created. This object is an empty physical file. In the next chapter you will enter data into this physical file, using the Data File Utility (DFU). When you have completely generated a data file, you will then be able to write programs or use utility software to read, change, and report on the data.

The AS/400 uses Data Description Specifications (DDSs) to define data attributes for external physical file descriptions. The field name, field length, data type (alphabetic or numeric), and other record information are defined with a DDS. The data description specification definition is contained within the AS/400's built-in database system and is therefore independent of any program. The advantage of this external file description is that multiple utility programs and application programs may utilize the DDS and process the data using the same record description.

In addition to field name, field length, and data type, other key words can be included that allow further definition of a field. The keyword COLHDG defines column headings that can be used by DFU and Query. The key words RANGE and VALUES define specific values that a field may contain that can be used for data validation by DFU. The keyword ERRMSG defines an error message to be displayed if certain conditions occur. Refer to the AS/400 DDS Reference manual for more information.

The AS/400's text editor, the Source Entry Utility (SEU), will be used to enter the physical file description source member. SEU is the AS/400 full screen editor that is used to work with any type of source code member. With SEU, new lines can be inserted, existing lines can be changed or deleted, lines can be moved from one place to another, and specific strings of characters within a member can be located. SEU also provides some syntax checking for each of the statements.

After the physical file record specification has been entered, this record specification will need to be compiled. Compiling checks each statement for syntax errors.

In this chapter you will again use the Programming Development Manager (PDM). PDM is a tool that will help you to develop and work with objects and members. PDM allows access to SEU and DFU, as well as files, message queues, and output queues.

**SOURCE
MEMBERS**

Access the **Work with Objects Using PDM** screen.

Type	wrkobjpdm	on any command line
Press	Enter	

See Figure 6.1.

```
                     Work with Objects Using PDM

     Library . . . . .   YOURNAME         Position to . . . . . . . .
                                          Position to type  . . . . .

     Type options, press Enter.
       2=Change       3=Copy        4=Delete      5=Display     7=Rename
       8=Display description         9=Save       10=Restore    11=Move ...

     Opt  Object     Type       Attribute   Text
     __   YOURNAME   *OUTQ                  Your Name OUTQ
     __   SOURCE     *FILE      PF-SRC      Your Name SOURCE
     __   YOURNAME   *JOBD                  Your Name JOB DESC




                                                                   Bottom
     Parameters or command
     ==>_____
     F3=Exit         F4=Prompt          F5=Refresh         F6=Create
     F9=Retrieve     F10=Command entry  F23=More options   F24=More keys
```

FIGURE 6.1   Work with Objects Using PDM

There are currently three objects in your library. Your output queue and job description were discussed in Chapter 5. The SOURCE object will be accessed for storing a physical file source member. Note that SOURCE has a type of *FILE, with an attribute of PF-SRC, a source physical file.

You will store all of the source code created as members within the object named SOURCE. These members may include physical and logical file descriptions, screen formats, and program code (COBOL, RPG, and so on). Therefore you will need to "Work with" your SOURCE object to access the individual members. Option 12 is used to access members within objects.

Type	12	in the Opt column prior to SOURCE
Press	Enter	

See Figure 6.2.

You are now working *within* your SOURCE file. The file name (SOURCE) and the library name (yourname) are at the top of the screen. This **Work with Members Using PDM** screen is where source members will be created and edited.

```
                        Work with Members Using PDM

 File . . . . . .    SOURCE
   Library . . . .   YOURNAME                 Position to . . . . .

 Type options, press Enter.
   2=Edit           3=Copy        4=Delete      5=Display      6=Print
   7=Rename         8=Display description       9=Save        13=Change text ...

 Opt  Member       Type          Text

   (No members in file)




 Parameters or command
 ==>_____
 F3=Exit          F4=Prompt        F5=Refresh          F6=Create
 F9=Retrieve      F10=Command entry F23=More options   F24=More keys
```

FIGURE 6.2   Work with Members Using PDM

CREATING A PHYSICAL FILE MEMBER WITH SEU

You are going to create an external physical file description for a payroll master file, which will be named PAYMST. This sample file will be used throughout this text to demonstrate various techniques. Each record will contain four fields: employee name and number, department number, and monthly salary.

The Source Entry Utility (SEU) will be used to enter and edit the data description specifications for the PAYMST source member in SOURCE. Look at the bottom of the **Work with Members Using PDM** screen and locate the function key list. F6 is the Create command key. This Create function will allow you to enter the new member name and its type and will transfer automatically to SEU.

Press	F6	to create a member

See Figure 6.3 for the **Start Source Entry Utility** screen.

SEU must be told what member and member type you want to create. The Source file name and Library name will not change. You need to put information into the next three fields. The Source member is the name of the physical file you are creating. The Source type tells SEU what type of code you will be entering, for example, PF (physical file), LF (logical file), CBL (COBOL), or RPG (RPG/400). SEU will provide the proper formats and syntax checking for the selected file type. The Text description will show on the **Work with Members Using PDM** screen to describe the member. The text description is not required but is highly recommended.

```
                         Start Source Entry Utility (STRSEU)

    Type choices, press Enter.

    Source file  . . . . . . . . . >  SOURCE        Name, *PRV
      Library  . . . . . . . . . . >  YOURNAME      Name, *LIBL, *CURLIB, *PRV
    Source member  . . . . . . . .    *PRV          Name, *PRV, *SELECT
    Source type  . . . . . . . . .    *SAME         Name, *SAME, BAS, BASP, C...
    Text 'description'  . . . . . .   *BLANK_____







                                                                          Bottom
    F3=Exit    F4=Prompt   F5=Refresh   F12=Cancel   F13=How to use this display
    F24=More keys
```

FIGURE 6.3   Start Source Entry Utiltiy

Type	PAYMST	in the Source member
Press	Field Exit	
Type	PF	in the Source type
Press	Field Exit	
Type	Payroll Master	in the Text description
	File Description	
Press	Enter	

The SEU edit screen is displayed in Figure 6.4.

SEU is the AS/400's general utility program to enter any source member code. The top right portion of the screen lists the library name and object file that holds this particular member. On the next line the member name is displayed. The center of the screen will hold the specifications or instructions. The lower part of the screen lists the function keys that may be used in SEU. The very bottom line should have the message that the member has been added to the SOURCE file within your library. This message confirms that the Create function completed normally. If you did not receive this message, press F3 and redo these instructions.

SEU is a full-screen line editor. It is similar to a word processor but more restrictive, since there is no word wrap feature. You will be entering lines of code, whether they are data description specifications or program instructions. SEU is aware of the type of source code as it was entered on the **Start SEU Utility** screen. SEU will do some minimal syntax checking.

```
    Columns . . . :   1  71              Edit              YOURNAME/SOURCE
    SEU==> _____         PAYMST
    FMT PF .....A..........T.Name++++++RLen++TDpB.....Functions++++++++++++++++
           *************** Beginning of data ********************************
    ,,,,,,,
    ,,,,,,,
    ,,,,,,,
    ,,,,,,,
    ,,,,,,,
    ,,,,,,,
    ,,,,,,,
    ,,,,,,,
    ,,,,,,,
    ,,,,,,,
    ,,,,,,,
    ,,,,,,,
    ,,,,,,,
    ,,,,,,,

           ***************** End of data ***************************************

    F3=Exit    F4=Prompt    F5=Refresh    F9=Retrieve    F10=Cursor
    F16=Repeat find          F17=Repeat change         F24=More keys
    Member PAYMST added to file YOURNAME/SOURCE.                            +
```

FIGURE 6.4   *SEU Edit Screen for Physical File*

SEU can be used free-form, since the cursor position is shown in the lower right-hand corner of the screen. Currently, the cursor is in row 5, column 9 of the **SEU Edit** screen. Free-form mode is often used for corrections and changes after the bulk of the information is entered. It is easier to use the SEU prompt mode when you are entering new lines, since SEU places a prompted format at the bottom of the screen.

When you are in the prompt mode, you can bypass fields that you do not require with the Field Exit or Tab keys. Do not press Enter until the line is completed. After you press Enter, the line will be moved to the top portion of the screen, a sequence number will be assigned to the line, and SEU will provide a blank prompt line in the lower portion of the screen. The sequence number is only for reference purposes. When lines are added to a source member, the source code will be renumbered automatically.

SEU Prompt for a Physical File
———

Begin working with SEU by compressing all of the blank lines from the SEU screen.

Press	Enter	to compress the blank lines

It is not necessary to compress the blank lines, but this is a convenient method to move the cursor to the correct location to begin inserting lines.

You will key the information using SEU prompt mode. Notice that the cursor location has been updated and the bottom of the screen shows row 4, column 1. Because the cursor is already positioned, you can begin inserting with the prompt mode.

Type	IP	in sequence number area of the Beginning of data line
Press	Enter	

The I stands for "Insert data lines," and the P requests that the source code be entered, using predefined prompts.

SEU will automatically divide the screen and display the PF (physical file) prompt on the lower portion of the screen. The completed lines will be on the upper portion of the screen with a blank prompt line ready for information. The screen will appear as shown in Figure 6.5.

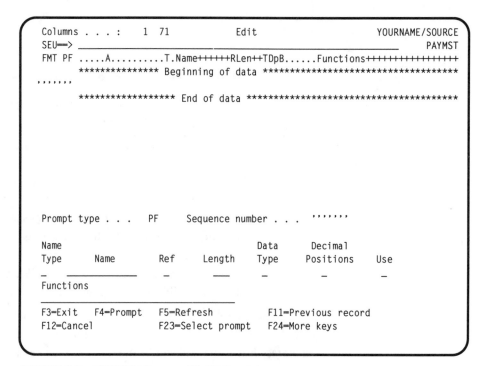

FIGURE 6.5   SEU Edit Screen with PF Prompt

The cursor will be located in the first field, which is the Name Type field. When you are typing, the cursor automatically moves to the next field if you have filled the entire length of a field. Otherwise, the Field Exit key should be used to align the characters in the field properly and move the cursor to the next field. If the field is an alphanumeric field, the characters will be aligned at the left edge of the field. If the field is numeric, the value will be right aligned. The Enter key is pressed only after all of the information for a line is correctly entered. All typing will be entered automatically in uppercase.

If you forget the Field Exit key or make other syntax errors, the field(s) in error will be highlighted on the prompt line, and the entire line will be highlighted in the upper portion of the screen. The Arrow keys and Backspace key can be used to make corrections. Remember that the Help key will give you appropriate information for the field.

Entering a Physical File Description for the Payroll Master File

You are creating a physical file record description for the Payroll Master File, PAYMST. This physical file description will contain a record name definition and four field definitions. The first entry will always be the record name entry, and the remaining entries will be the field name entries. The fields must be defined as to the type of data that each will contain. Alphanumeric data fields must be defined with a data type code of A. Numeric data fields will be defined with a data type code of S, for signed numeric. There are other data type codes that can be used. Refer to the AS/400 Data Description Specification manual for more information.

The example Payroll Master File fields used in this text are:

Employee ID number: four alphanumeric characters
Department number: three alphanumeric characters
Employee name: 20 alphanumeric characters
Monthly salary amount: six numeric characters with two decimal positions
    (9999.99)

The record name entry will need an R (for record format name) in the Name Type field. The record format name should be different from the file name. It is the authors' recommended naming convention to use the name of the physical file with an R appended to it. This is not an AS/400 requirement.

Type	R	in the Name Type field
Type	PAYMSTR	in the Name field
Press	Enter	

These are the only two entries that are required for this line. As soon as you press the Enter key on any line, the information is moved to the upper portion of the screen and given a sequence number. At the same time the lower portion of the screen is cleared for more source code entry.

A blank in the Name Type field will specify that this line is a field name, and its attributes will follow. Use Figure 6.6 as a guide for the first field name entry.

Press	Field Exit	to bypass the Name Type field
Type	EMPID	in the Name field
Press	Field Exit	
Press	Field Exit	to bypass the Ref field
Type	4	in the Length field
Press	Field Exit	
Type	A	in the Data Type field
Press	Field Exit	to bypass the Decimal Position field
Press	Field Exit	to bypass the Use field
Type	COLHDG('EMP ID')	in the Functions field
Press	Enter	

```
 Columns . . . :   1  71              Edit            YOURNAME/SOURCE
 SEU==>                                                        PAYMST
 FMT PF .....A..........T.Name++++++RLen++TDpB.....Functions+++++++++++++++
        *************** Beginning of data ********************************
 0001.00      A         R PAYMSTR
 .......

          ***************** End of data *********************************




 Prompt type . . .   PF      Sequence number . . .  .......

 Name                                      Data    Decimal
 Type       Name          Ref    Length    Type    Positions    Use
 _         EMPID____      _        _4      A          _          _
 Functions
 COLHDG('EMPID')_____
 F3=Exit  F4=Prompt    F5=Refresh        F11=Previous record
 F12=Cancel            F23=Select prompt  F24=More keys
```

FIGURE 6.6   SEU Edit Screen with PF Data

The column heading field has information that will be used by DFU and other utility programs. The abbreviation for column heading is COLHDG. The actual information that will be printed above the column must be enclosed in parentheses. If the column heading information is alphanumeric, it must be enclosed in single quotes within the parentheses.

Continue to enter the field information as shown in Figure 6.7. If you make any mistakes by pressing the wrong key, Appendix B contains a list of helpful information on SEU.

Variable names are no longer than six characters so that this external file description can be used in an RPG program. Other languages allow longer variable names.

FIGURE 6.7   Payroll Master File Field Information for DDS

Name Type	Name	Fld Len	Data Type	Dec Pos	Functions
R	PAYMSTR				
	EMPID	4	A		COLHDG('EMP ID')
	DEPTNO	3	A		COLHDG('DEPT NO')
	NAME	20	A		COLHDG('EMPLOYEE NAME')
	MONSAL	6	S	2	COLHDG('MONTHLY SALARY')

SEU EXIT **AND SAVE**	When all the entries have been keyed,

Press	F3	to exit SEU

Figure 6.8 will be displayed.

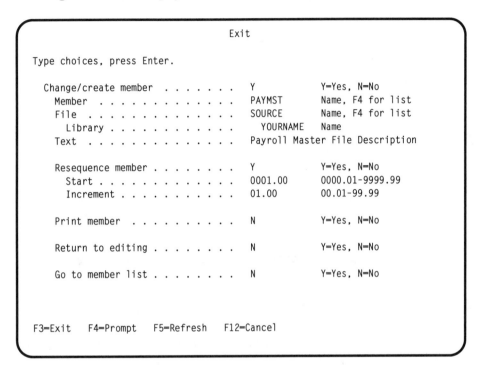

```
                                    Exit

 Type choices, press Enter.

     Change/create member  . . . . . . .    Y            Y=Yes, N=No
        Member  . . . . . . . . . . . .     PAYMST       Name, F4 for list
        File  . . . . . . . . . . . . .     SOURCE       Name, F4 for list
          Library . . . . . . . . . . .       YOURNAME   Name
        Text  . . . . . . . . . . . . .     Payroll Master File Description

     Resequence member . . . . . . . .      Y            Y=Yes, N=No
        Start . . . . . . . . . . . .       0001.00      0000.01-9999.99
        Increment . . . . . . . . . .       01.00        00.01-99.99

     Print member  . . . . . . . . . .      N            Y=Yes, N=No

     Return to editing . . . . . . . .      N            Y=Yes, N=No

     Go to member list . . . . . . . .      N            Y=Yes, N=No



 F3=Exit    F4=Prompt    F5=Refresh    F12=Cancel
```

FIGURE 6.8   *SEU Exit from PAYMST*

The default is set to Yes to Change/create a member. Read this screen and note that the PAYMST member will be stored in the SOURCE file within your library. Also notice the other Exit options, which are set to default values. The member will be resequenced automatically beginning with 1, incremented by 1. The member will not be printed. You will not be returned to editing. You will not go to the member list. Any of these options can be changed when you exit SEU.

Press	Enter	to save the definition and accept the defaults

You will now be returned to the **Work with Members Using PDM** screen. Note the message to verify that a member has been added to your library, as shown in Figure 6.9.

COMPILING A **PHYSICAL FILE** **SOURCE MEMBER**	A physical file source member cannot contain data. This source member must be compiled to create an empty physical file. A physical file is an object with a type of *FILE, and an attribute of PF-DTA. The compiling process checks the data description specification syntax to ensure that the source code syntax is correct and in a valid format. If the source code is correct, the compiler creates an empty physical file.

```
                        Work with Members Using PDM

  File . . . . . .     SOURCE
    Library . . . .    YOURNAME              Position to  . . . . .

  Type options, press Enter.
    2=Edit            3=Copy        4=Delete       5=Display      6=Print
    7=Rename          8=Display description        9=Save         13=Change text ...

  Opt  Member    Type       Text
    _   PAYMST    PF         Payroll Master File Description






                                                                    Bottom
    Parameters or command
    ===> _____
    F3=Exit          F4=Prompt          F5=Refresh          F6=Create
    F9=Retrieve      F10=Command entry  F23=More options    F24=More keys
    Member PAYMST added to file YOURNAME/SOURCE.                      +
```

FIGURE 6.9　**Work with Members Using PDM**

Press	F23	to display more options

Note that option 14 will initiate the compile process.

Type	14	in the option column before the member PAYMST
Press	Enter	to begin the compile process to create the physical file object

The compile process is a batch job. Notice the message "Job xxxxxx/userid/PAYMST submitted to job queue QBATCH in library QGPL" at the bottom of the screen. This system message notifies you that the physical file description PAYMST has been submitted to a system job queue called QBATCH in a system library called QGPL.

When the batch compile job has completed, you will receive a system informational message. The "torn corner" indicator will appear on the message line of your screen. To view the message,

Type	DSPMSG	on the command line
Press	Enter	

T I P　　**A shortcut to display messages is to type DM (display message) in any option column of your current screen and press Enter.**

The message will say that the compile completed normally or abnormally. If the compile ended abnormally, you will need to look at the report from the compiler to determine the problem(s). In either case, to access the compiler output and work with your output queue,

Type	12	in the option column before the output queue
Press	Enter	

A shortcut to reach your spooled file output is to type SP in any option column of your current screen and press Enter.

You will see a spooled file named PAYMST listed. When you display the contents of this file on the screen, any syntax errors will appear at the end of the listing. You will know from your message whether there was a "clean" compile. The compiler output contains the source code member and other expanded compiler information about the data description specifications. Use the Shift/Roll keys to scroll through the listing.

Type	5	in the option column before the spooled output
Press	Enter	
Press	Shift/Roll Up	to locate any messages

Correcting Source Code
———

If there are any errors in your source code, the errors must be corrected. Compare your source member code to the Payroll Master File Field Information for DDS in Figure 6.7. Verify that the field length, names, and data types match the text. In the next chapter we will enter data into this empty physical file, and this format is expected.

To correct the physical file description, you will need to edit your SOURCE member, PAYMST. On the **Work with Members Using PDM** screen you will see the physical file source member PAYMST. The edit option will return to SEU and will bring in the previously saved description to allow editing of any source member. Appendix B contains a list of helpful information on SEU, and Appendix C contains information on split-screen editing.

Type	2	to edit the source member
Press	F3	when you have completed the changes
Type	14	to recompile the physical file according to the previous instructions

COMPILED OBJECTS

When the source member PAYMST was compiled, an object named PAYMST was created. The new object is a *FILE type object with an attribute of PF-DTA.

Press	F12	to return to the **Work with Objects Using PDM** screen

Your screen should look like Figure 6.10.

```
                      Work with Objects Using PDM

   Library . . . . .   YOURNAME          Position to . . . . . . . .
                                         Position to type . . . . .

   Type options, press Enter.
     2=Change         3=Copy        4=Delete      5=Display      7=Rename
     8=Display description          9=Save        10=Restore     11=Move ...

   Opt  Object      Type       Attribute    Text
   __   YOURNAME    *OUTQ                    Your Name OUTQ
   __   PAYMST      *FILE      PF-DTA        Payroll Master File Description
   __   SOURCE      *FILE      PF-SRC        Your Name SOURCE
   __   YOURNAME    *JOBD                    Your Name JOB DESC




                                                                  Bottom
   Parameters or command
   ===>_____
   F3=Exit          F4=Prompt           F5=Refresh          F6=Create
   F9=Retrieve      F10=Command entry    F23=More options    F24=More keys
```

FIGURE 6.10   Work with Objects Using PDM

T I P   When you return to the **Work with Objects Using PDM** screen, the file **PAYMST**
             might not be displayed. Press F5 to refresh the screen.

Type	12	in the option column before PAYMST to work with the *FILE
Press	Enter	

The "Work with" option displays a screen to confirm that this object has no
members. You will create a member for the PAYMST physical file in the next chapter
by entering data into PAYMST using DFU.

Press	F12	to return to the previous screen

RECOMPILING A SOURCE MEMBER

When an object already exists and a source member is recompiled, a **Confirm Compile
of Member** screen appears, as shown in Figure 6.11. To access this screen, recompile
your PAYMST source member. You have the option to delete the existing object for this
member. You must respond Y, for yes, to create a new object.

Type	12	in the option column prior to SOURCE
Type	14	in the option column to compile the source member, PAYMST
Type	y	to delete the existing object

```
                        Confirm Compile of Member

The following object already exists for the compile operation:

   Object which exists  . . . . . . . . :     PAYMST
      Library  . . . . . . . . . . . . . :       YOURNAME
   Object type  . . . . . . . . . . . . :     *FILE

   Member to compile  . . . . . . . . . :     PAYMST
   File . . . . . . . . . . . . . . . . :     SOURCE
      Library  . . . . . . . . . . . . . :       YOURNAME

Type choice, press Enter.
Press F12=Cancel to return and not perform the compile operation.

   Delete existing object . . . . . . . .     N    Y=Yes, N=No






F12=Cancel
```

FIGURE 6.11   Confirm Compile of Member

Do not change the physical file description and recompile once you have data in the file! If this becomes necessary, see your instructor for the necessary steps, or you will lose your data!

SUMMARY

1. To create an external physical file description, you must complete the following steps:

    a. Work with SOURCE to access the **Work with Members Using PDM** screen.
    b. Press F6 to create a new member.
    c. Enter the new member name, type, and description.
    d. Code the record and field descriptions for the physical file, using SEU.
    e. Press F3 to Exit and Save the entries.
    f. Compile the source member using option 14.
    g. If not correct, change the source member by entering option 2 (Edit) to work in SEU. Repeat steps e and f.

2. When a source member is recompiled after an object already exists, a **Confirm Compile of Member** screen appears. You have the option to delete the existing object for this source member. You must respond Y, for yes, to create a new object; otherwise, the AS/400 will terminate the compile process. Data is entered into the physical file object.

3. To access SEU:

    a. To create a new member, press F6 on the **Work with Members Using PDM** screen.
    b. To change a member, place a 2 in the Opt column.

REVIEW QUESTIONS

1. Why are physical files described externally from their application programs on the AS/400?

2. What is the purpose of SEU?

3. How is SEU able to help syntax check the source member that is being entered?

4. When the source member PAYMST was compiled, an object with the same name was created. Where was that object placed in your library?

EXERCISES

1. Using the process defined in this chapter, create a physical file description for a Department Master File. The source member name will be DPTMST, with a source type of PF and a text description of Department Master File Description.

```
DEPARTMENT MASTER FILE FIELD INFORMATION
Name              Fld  Data Dec
Type Name         Len  Type Pos  Functions
R    DPTMSTR
     DPTNO        3    A         COLHDG('DEPT NO')
     DPTNAME      20   A         COLHDG('DEPT NAME')
     DPTBUDG      7    S    0    COLHDG('ANNUAL BUDGET')
```

Print the compiler output and verify that the field information is correct. The spooled file name will be DPTMST.

2. Using the process defined in this chapter, create a physical file description for an Employee Address File. The source member name will be ADRMST, with a source type of PF and a text description of Employee Address Master File Description.

```
ADDRESS MASTER FILE FIELD INFORMATION
Name              Fld  Data Dec
Type Name         Len  Type Pos  Functions
R    ADRMSTR
     EMPID        4    A         COLHDG('EMP ID')
     STREET       20   A         COLHDG('STREET')
     CITY         15   A         COLHDG('CITY')
     STATE        2    A         COLHDG('STATE')
     ZIP          5    A         COLHDG('ZIP CD')
     PHONE        10   A         COLHDG('PHONE NO')
```

Print the compiler output and verify that the field information is correct. The spooled file name will be ADRMST.

3. Access the spooled files in your output queue. Delete any files that you will not be printing.

4. For additional information on AS/400 files, review the online tutorial *How Database Is Implemented on the System*.

CHAPTER SEVEN

Entering Data into a Physical File

To learn how to access the Data File Utility (DFU).

To understand the process of entering data
into a physical file.

INTRODUCTION

A physical file source member was created and compiled in the previous chapter. Data will now be added into the empty physical file object, PAYMST. A COBOL or RPG program could be written to add data, but the AS/400 has a utility program that is available to perform this function. The Data File Utility (DFU) can be used to add data into any existing file. This utility can also be used to change or correct data in an existing file. For more information on DFU, see the AS/400 DFU User's Guide and Reference manual.

DFU can create temporary specifications or can save the specifications to create a permanent program. The DFU specifications are used to enter or change data in a physical file. DFU provides a fast and easy method to accomplish this task. In a working environment there would be very few DFU programs for production data files, since it has limited editing and error message capabilities. Keying errors, omission of data, and incorrect data are accepted by DFU. Additionally, DFU provides a poor audit trail. In the workplace, each system would control file changes by validating the data, by limiting the number of people who are authorized to modify the data, by allowing only certain changes by specific departments, or by requiring authorization to modify fields. All of these methods can be provided by programs that verify data accuracy, check user authorities, and provide a report that monitors the changes.

In a student environment there is not sufficient time to write one or more programs to capture data. Therefore this chapter will accept the limitations of DFU and employ the utility software to enter data. DFU is used in industry to create and update test data files, just as you will be doing.

USING THE DATA FILE UTILITY (DFU)

An object PAYMST of type *FILE was created when the source member PAYMST was compiled in the last chapter. The *FILE is a physical file with an attribute of PF-DTA. This physical file is empty and ready to accept data. Access the **Work with Objects Using PDM** menu. See Figure 7.1.

TIP

You can key WRKOBJPDM on any command line.

Press	F23	to see more options

Note that option 18 is to Change using DFU. This option will create a temporary Data File Utility program to enter data into the empty physical file, PAYMST. This option can also be used to correct the data, add more records, or delete records. Option 18 will create the DFU program specifications, allow you to run them, and then delete the DFU specifications when you have completed entering the data.

Type	18	in the option column in front of PAYMST
Press	Enter	

```
                        Work with Objects Using PDM                    .

    Library . . . . .    YOURNAME          Position to . . . . . . . .
                                           Position to type  . . . . .

    Type options, press Enter.
      2=Change        3=Copy        4=Delete        5=Display      7=Rename
      8=Display description          9=Save         10=Restore     11=Move ...

    Opt   Object      Type       Attribute   Text
    __    YOURNAME    *OUTQ                   Your Name OUTQ
    __    PAYMST      *FILE      PF-DTA       Payroll Master File Description
    __    SOURCE      *FILE      PF-SRC       Your Name SOURCE
    __    YOURNAME    *JOBD                   Your Name JOB DESC



                                                                      Bottom
    Parameters or command
    ==>_____
    F3=Exit          F4=Prompt            F5=Refresh          F6=Create
    F9=Retrieve      F10=Command entry     F23=More options    F24=More keys
```

FIGURE 7.1   Work with Objects Using PDM

If the Create function proceeds normally, DFU will display the following system message on the bottom of the screen while it is creating the program: "DFU is creating Temporary Program QDZTD00001 for you to run." DFU will display the data entry screen, as shown in Figure 7.2.

```
    WORK WITH DATA IN A FILE            Mode . . . . :   ENTRY
    Format . . . . :   PAYMSTR          File . . . . :   PAYMST


    EMP ID:          ____
    DEPT NO:         __
    EMPLOYEE NAME:   _____
    MONTHLY SALARY:  _____








    F3=Exit          F5=Refresh              F6=Select format
    F9=Insert        F10=Entry               F11=Change
                                          (C) COPYRIGHT IBM CORP. 1980, 1991.
```

FIGURE 7.2   DFU Data Entry Screen

DFU will begin in the Entry mode. Entry mode will always add new records to the end of the physical file and does not allow changes to existing records. However, by utilizing the function keys, changes can be made to existing records without exiting DFU. The end of this chapter has a section named DFU TIPS with more information on the function keys.

Look at Figure 7.2 and note the following information. The format name, PAYMSTR, is the record name of the source member. The file name is the physical file, PAYMST. This screen lists the column heading (COLHDG) names that were defined for the fields in the physical file description. The column headings are shown on the left edge of the screen. The next entry on each line is a highlighted area where the data will be entered for each field in the PAYMST file. The highlighted area is the field length that was defined by using the Data Description Specification (DDS).

To move to the next field after entering data, use the Field Exit key. Use the Backspace, Delete, and Arrow keys to correct keying errors. Do not press the Enter key until all fields have been completed and any keying errors have been corrected. Once the Enter key has been pressed, the data will be placed into the file, and the screen will be cleared in preparation for the next record.

Now enter the data as shown in Figure 7.3. Enter all six digits for the monthly salary, but do not enter decimals in the monthly salary amount. The decimal was defined in DDS when you defined the field length as six with two decimal positions. The decimal position is assumed, and the decimal point is an invalid character in a numeric field. Enter all the data in uppercase to facilitate later options.

Press	Shift Lock	to type in uppercase

When you have completed entering the data,

Press	F3	to exit DFU

Figure 7.4 shows the total number of records added, changed, or deleted.

FIGURE 7.3	**PAYMST Data**

EMP ID	DEPT NO	EMPLOYEE NAME	MONTHLY SALARY
1234	400	JONES, BILL	132200
3567	600	SMITHE, CAROL	156775
5632	200	GREEN, TOM	120000
2567	100	ADAMS, MARK	154650
4672	600	BLACKBERG, KAREN	130000
7290	400	KLEIN, JOHN	140000
1892	500	TUCKER, MARY	150000
0516	400	WALKER, GARY	177525
6340	100	POWERS, SUSAN	172500
5718	300	HART, BOB	122200

```
                              End Data Entry

     Number of records processes

          Added  . . . . . :          10
          Changed  . . . . :           0
          Deleted  . . . . :           0




     Type choice, press Enter.

       End data entry . . . . . . .    Y          Y=Yes,  N=No







     F3=Exit       F12=Cancel
     All records added, changed, or deleted will be printed.
```

FIGURE 7.4   End DFU Data Entry

All records added, changed, or deleted will be printed. Ensure that all the records have been entered into the physical file. If there are fewer than ten records, type N, press Enter, and continue keying the records.

Verify	10 records	are added

Answer Y or N depending on the number of records added; if no, make appropriate corrections.

Press	Enter	when all records are added

Work with the data in PAYMST.

Type	12	in the option column before PAYMST
Press	Enter	

See Figure 7.5 for the **Work with Members Using PDM** screen.

To view the data in this physical file member,

Type	5	in the option column to display the data in the physical file member
Press	Enter	

See Figure 7.6 for the correct data.

The display of a physical file member is in the format of the physical file description. Data is in the positions that were specified in the Data Description Specification (DDS) with no blanks between the fields, exactly as it is stored on disk.

```
                    Work with Members Using PDM

File . . . . . .    PAYMST
   Library . . . .    YOURNAME              Position to . . . . ____

Type options, press Enter.
   3=Copy    4=Delete       5=Display   7=Rename    8=Display description
   9=Same    13=Change text  18=Change using DFU   25=Find string

Opt  Member     Date        Text
 __   PAYMST     02/02/92    Payroll Master File Description




                                                              Bottom
Parameters or command
===>_____
F3=Exit         F4=Prompt            F5=Refresh         F6=Create
F9=Retrieve     F10=Command entry                       F24=More keys
```

FIGURE 7.5   Work with Members Using PDM

```
                    Display Physical File Member
File . . . . . . :  PAYMST          Library . . . . :  YOURNAME
Member . . . . . :  PAYMST          Record . . . . . :  1
Control . . . . :   _____      Column . . . . . :  1
Find . . . . . . :   _____
*...+....1....+....2....+....3...
1234400JONES, BILL          132200
3567600SMITHE, CAROL        156775
5632200GREEN, TOM           120000
2567100ADAMS, MARK          154650
4672600BLACKBERG, KAREN     130000
7290400KLEIN, JOHN          140000
1892500TUCKER, MARY         150000
0516400WALKER, GARY         177525
6340100POWERS, SUSAN        172500
5718300HART, BOB            122200
                      ****** END OF DATA ******




                                                              Bottom
F3=Exit    F12=Cancel   F19=Left   F20=Right   F24=More keys
```

FIGURE 7.6   Display Physical File Member PAYMST

| Press | F12 | to return to the **Work with Members Using PDM** screen |
| Press | F12 | to return to the **Work with Objects Using PDM** screen |

DFU has placed an Audit Log of all data entries in your output queue. To look at this file,

| Type | 12 | in the option column before the output queue |
| Press | Enter | |

T I P **Or type WRKSPLF on the command line or SP on an option line.**

The spooled file output from DFU has a file name of QPDZDTALOG, a data log that was generated by a system utility.

| Type | 5 | in the option column to display the log |

Compare your work to Figure 7.7 and verify that your data entry is correct.

```
                          Display Spooled File
  File  . . . . . :  QPDZDTALOG                    Page/Line   1/1
  Control . . . . .  _____                    Columns    1 - 78
  Find  . . . . . .  _____
  *...+....1....+....2....+....3....+....4....+....5....+....6....+....7....+...
   5738SS1    V2R1M0  910524                              AUDIT LOG
    Library/File . . . . .   YOURNAME/PAYMST
    Member . . . . . . . .   PAYMST
    Job Title  . . . . . .   WORK WITH DATA IN A FILE
                     RECNBR     EMP ID DEPT NO EMPLOYEE NAME      MONTHLY SALA
  Added                  1       1234    400   JONES, BILL           1322.00
  Added                  2       3567    600   SMITHE, CAROL         1567.75
  Added                  3       5632    200   GREEN, TOM            1200.00
  Added                  4       2567    100   ADAMS, MARK           1546.50
  Added                  5       4672    600   BLACKBERG, KAREN      1300.00
  Added                  6       7290    400   KLEIN, JOHN           1400.00
  Added                  7       1892    500   TUCKER, MARY          1500.00
  Added                  8       0516    400   WALKER, GARY          1775.25
  Added                  9       6340    100   POWERS, SUSAN         1725.00
  Added                 10       5718    300   HART, BOB             1222.00
               10   Records Added
                                                                    More...
  F3=Exit    F12=Cancel   F19=Left    F20=Right    F24=More keys
```

FIGURE 7.7 Display Spooled File from DFU

Print this spooled file.

DFU **CHANGE MODE**

If you made a keying error, have an extra record, or left out a record from the Payroll Master File, these errors can be corrected. Start DFU using option 18 on the PAYMST object. Because this file has existing records, DFU is automatically switched into the Change mode. See Figure 7.8.

```
WORK WITH DATA IN A FILE                      Mode . . . . :   CHANGE
Format . . . . :   PAYMSTR                    File . . . . :   PAYMST

   *RECNBR:   _____













   F3=Exit                 F5=Refresh              F6=Select format
   F9=Insert               F10=Entry               F11=Change
                                         (C) COPYRIGHT IBM CORP. 1980, 1991.
```

FIGURE 7.8   DFU Change Screen

DFU assigns a relative record number to each record in the order that the records were entered. Relative record numbers mean that the first record entered is assigned a number 1, the second record is number 2, and so forth. The relative record number (*RECNBR) will be displayed next to each record on your output list from DFU. See Figure 7.7 for a list of the relative record numbers. If you need to change a record, enter the record number, press Field Exit, and press Enter.

As an example, access the first record in the file.

Type	1	in the *RECNBR field
Press	Field Exit	to align the value 1
Press	Enter	

The first record will be displayed as shown in Figure 7.9.

Because this file is not a keyed file, all records are added at the end of the file. This sequential mode is called arrival sequence. If you wish to add a record, press F9 to change to Insert mode or F10 to change to Entry mode. You will see a blank data entry screen.

```
WORK WITH DATA IN A FILE                Mode . . . . :    CHANGE
Format . . . . :    PAYMSTR             File . . . . :    PAYMST

*RECNBR:                   1
EMP ID:         1234
DEPT NO:        400
EMPLOYEE NAME:  JONES, BILL
MONTHLY SALARY: 132200




F3=Exit              F5=Refresh           F6=Select format
F9=Insert            F10=Entry            F11=Change
```

FIGURE 7.9   DFU Change Screen for Record 1 in PAYMST

If you need to delete a record, the record to be deleted must first be displayed on your screen. Enter the relative record number, press Field Exit, and press Enter. Confirm that the record you want to delete is the one on your screen. Press F23 to initiate the delete process. You will be asked to confirm the delete request by pressing F23 again.

Press	F3	to exit DFU and return to the **Work with Objects Using PDM** screen

Each time DFU is exited, an Audit Log is created. Therefore if you made corrections after saving, there will be more than one QPDZDTALOG spooled file.

SUMMARY OF THE PROCESS OF CREATING A PHYSICAL FILE WITH DATA

In the previous chapter you began the process of creating a physical file to contain data. With the AS/400 operating system this process contains many steps.

The following outline reviews the file creation process.

1. Use the WRKOBJPDM command to obtain a list of all the objects within your library.

2. Type a 12 in the option column prior to the *FILE named SOURCE to "Work with" SOURCE. New physical file description source members are placed within SOURCE.

3. The screen is now **Work with Members Using PDM**. The operating system will place the new member within the SOURCE file. Press F6 to create a new source member.

4. Fill in the Source member name and a Source member type of physical file (pf), and provide a Description stating the file's purpose.

5. You are now in the Source Entry Utility (SEU). The Data Description Specifications (DDS) must now be entered for the physical file.

6. Type an R in the Name Type field. Type the file name with an R appended to the end in the Name field. These entries create the record format name.

7. Enter each field with a descriptive name. Field names should be no longer than six characters to function properly in both RPG/400 and COBOL. Each field requires both a field length and a data type. Common data types are A for alphanumeric data, S for signed numeric data, and P for packed numeric data. Although not required, fields should be assigned column headings at this time for use in DFU and Query. Press F3 to exit and save the description.

8. Now that the member has been saved, it must be compiled. Type a 14 in the option column before the member name.

9. When the "torn corner" graphic appears on the bottom of the screen, type a dm in any option column. The message will state whether the compile completed normally or abnormally. If there were errors, correct the mistakes and recompile the member.

10. When the member has compiled correctly, there will be a *FILE object with the same name as the member on the **Work with Objects Using PDM** menu. This object is now ready to contain data.

11. To enter data into the object, type an 18 in the option column to begin the Data File Utility (DFU) program. The operating system will display the message "DFU is creating Temporary Program QDZTD0001 for you to run."

12. Enter the data that is appropriate for each record in the file. Use the Field Exit key to move from field to field within a record. Use the Enter key only when all the fields for a record have been entered correctly.

13. Exit DFU with F3. To check the accuracy of the data entry, type SP in any option column and display the spooled Audit Log that resulted from the data entry. This should also be printed.

HELPFUL CL COMMANDS FOR FILES

If the data has been entered by some other person or at a previous time or the DFU Audit Log has been deleted from the print queue, use the DSPPFM (Display physical file member) command to view the data file. See Chapter 10 for more information on this command.

To print any physical file member, use the CPYF (Copy file) command with *PRINT as the To File name. See Chapter 10 for more information on this command.

DFU TIPS	There are more function keys available on most DFU screens than are shown on the bottom of the screen. Below is a list of the most useful keys and what operation each performs. Using the Arrow keys, place the cursor on the function key area and press Help to learn more about each key.

F5 = REFRESH	Press F5 to remove any changes made on the screen and see the original values stored on the disk. This works only prior to pressing Enter.
F9 = INSERT	Press F9 to switch to Insert mode from either Entry or Change mode. Inserted records are added at the end of a sequential (nonkeyed) file. In a keyed file, inserted records are added at the current key position.
F10 = ENTRY	Press F10 to switch to Entry mode from Change mode or Insert mode. In Entry mode a new record is added at the end of the file.
F11 = CHANGE	Press F11 to switch to Change mode from Entry mode or Insert mode. Existing records are displayed and available to be changed in this mode.
F23 = DELETE A RECORD	You must be in Change mode to delete a record. Press F23 to delete the record currently displayed on the screen. You will receive a message to press F23 again to confirm that you want to delete the record.

REVIEW QUESTIONS	1. Explain the use of DFU in a business environment.
	2. Explain the use of DFU in a student environment.
	3. Why is the data on a **Display Physical File Member** screen not formatted with spaces?
	4. List the major steps to create a physical file with data.

EXERCISES	1. Enter the following data into the DPTMST physical file that was created in Chapter 5.

DEPT NO	DEPT NAME	ANNUAL BUDGET
600	ADMINISTRATION	150,000
100	ACCOUNTING	75,000
500	MAINTENANCE	67,000
200	PAYROLL	342,500
400	COMPUTER SERVICES	50,000
300	PERSONNEL	56,000

Print the Audit Log.

2. Enter the following data into the ADRMST physical file that was created in Chapter 5.

EMP ID	STREET	CITY	STATE	ZIP	PHONE
7290	610 WASHINGTON #6	BOSTON	MA	01002	6175339876
5718	7353 ADAMS AVE	PORTLAND	OR	97801	5038771275
1234	639 JEFFERSON #110	BOSTON	MA	01021	6175320888
2567	8462 CARTER BLVD	PORTLAND	OR	97811	5038774561
5632	4549 MADISON AVE	BOSTON	MA	01022	6175334702
3567	784 MONROE	PORTLAND	OR	97822	5038769455
4672	8462 JACKSON	BOSTON	MA	01022	6175338483
1892	8562 VAN BUREN	PORTLAND	OR	97827	5038763260
3516	4345 TYLER	BOSTON	MA	01025	6175331111
6340	2698 POLK	PORTLAND	OR	97812	5038773828

Print the Audit Log.

3. Access the spooled files in your output queue. Delete any files that you will not be printing.

CHAPTER EIGHT

Access Paths and Introduction to Logical Files

To understand the purpose of an access path.

To be able to create a logical file.

INTRODUCTION TO ACCESS PATHS

In previous chapters the PAYMST physical file was created, and data was entered into this file. Programs are written or utility software is used to report on data files. The sequence of the data in a physical file is often not what is needed for a report. The AS/400 access path describes the order in which records are read by programs or utility software. There are two access paths: arrival sequence and keyed sequence.

PAYMST is an arrival sequence file. No key field was specified for the records in the physical file description, and therefore the records are stored in the order in which the data was entered. Arrival sequence is usually not a meaningful sequence. Therefore records must be resequenced on a field, such as name or department number, for a report to be useful. To read records in an order other than the arrival sequence requires establishing one or more key fields. The records are then accessed in the sequence of the named keyed fields.

Resequencing data into a productive order is essential in the business environment. Access paths to resequence data can be generated with two methods. The first method is the use of a logical file. This is the topic of this chapter. The second method of generating access paths is to use the Query/400 utility software. This is the topic of the next chapter.

ACCESS PATHS VIA LOGICAL FILES

A logical file contains no data. A logical file is a description of how data is to be read or written to disk by a program. A logical file access path is used by high-level languages such as RPG, COBOL, Pascal, or CL. The logical file is not a precreated index. The access path of the logical file is created each time it is used. Physical files are constantly being updated. A program using a logical file will always be using the latest version of the physical files that the logical file references.

A logical file can be used to resequence a physical file, such as listing a file in name sequence rather than social security number sequence. Multiple key fields can be used to sequence a file.

A logical file can also be used to reduce the number of fields available to a program. For example, it may be advantageous to have department secretaries update the payroll file's address fields. However, it is not acceptable to have each department secretary change the salary data. A logical file could be created to limit access to fields. This logical file would contain only the fields necessary for address changes. The physical file would still contain all of the fields to run payroll, and security would be maintained.

Another use of logical files is to join one or more files in a relation. If you have been doing the exercises at the end of the chapters, you now have three physical files in your library: PAYMST, DPTMST, and ADRMST. These files can be joined on common fields. The PAYMST and ADRMST files have a common employee id field. The PAYMST and DPTMST files have a common department number field. Joining would be required for a report that lists employee name, employee address, and the department name. For more information on logical files and joins, see the Data Description Specifications reference manual.

RELATIONSHIP OF PHYSICAL FILES TO LOGICAL FILES

Before creating a logical file, we will review physical files. We will use a display of the physical file description of PAYMST for the review. Because physical file descriptions are members of the SOURCE file, accessing the **Work with Members Using PDM** screen is required.

Type	WRKMBRPDM	on a command line
Press	Enter	

Locate the physical file description for PAYMST.

Type	5	in the appropriate option column
Press	Enter	

Figure 8.1 will now be displayed on your screen.

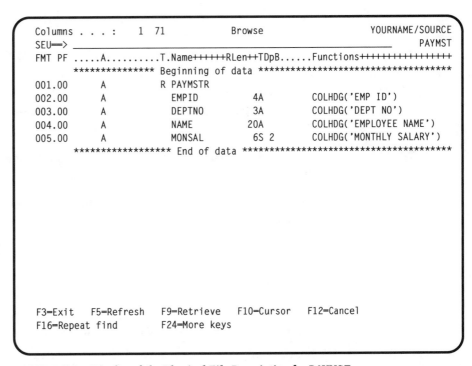

```
Columns . . . :   1  71              Browse              YOURNAME/SOURCE
SEU==>  _____        PAYMST
FMT PF .....A..........T.Name++++++RLen++TDpB......Functions+++++++++++++++++
        *************** Beginning of data *********************************
001.00      A          R PAYMSTR
002.00      A            EMPID        4A           COLHDG('EMP ID')
003.00      A            DEPTNO       3A           COLHDG('DEPT NO')
004.00      A            NAME        20A           COLHDG('EMPLOYEE NAME')
005.00      A            MONSAL       6S 2         COLHDG('MONTHLY SALARY')
        ***************** End of data *************************************




        F3=Exit   F5=Refresh   F9=Retrieve   F10=Cursor   F12=Cancel
        F16=Repeat find        F24=More keys
```

FIGURE 8.1   Display of the Physical File Description for PAYMST

The physical file description has several items that are important in creating a logical file. The first line is the record name, which is denoted by the R prior to the record name. In this text the record name is the file name plus the character R to note its status as a record name. Thus the record name is PAYMSTR. The same physical file record name is a required entry when creating a logical file.

For a physical file, all of the field names are listed below the record name. The logical file description will require only the fields that will be needed in the program that will use logical files. Data fields in the physical file are linked to the logical file definition through the PFILE parameter.

Press	F12	to cancel the display and return to the WRKMBRPDM screen

Figure 8.2 shows the flow of control from the physical file to the finished report.

Programs that use a logical file specify only the logical file name. No reference is made to the physical file except in the logical file description.

CREATING A LOGICAL FILE

A logical file will now be created to allow programs to access the PAYMST physical file in a keyed sequence. A report requires the data to be in order by department number and then alphabetically by employee name (or employee name within department). The key fields associated with this logical file will be DEPTNO and NAME.

Create a new source member for the logical file.

Press	F6	to begin the creation

The logical file source member will be named PAYMSTL1. The similarity in file names helps a programmer connect this logical file to the physical file. The L states that it is a logical file, and the number 1 states that it is the first logical file for the PAYMST physical file. The source type LF defines this source member as a logical file. The AS/400 operating system has over 30 different source types.

T I P

To see a list of source types, place the cursor on the source type line and press the Help key.

The entries of the source member name, the source type, and the text description should be as follows.

Type	PAYMSTL1	for source member
Press	Field Exit	
Type	LF	for the source type
Press	Field Exit	
Type	PAYMST in sequence by dept, name	for the descriptive text

---

FIGURE 8.2   ***Logical File Linkage***

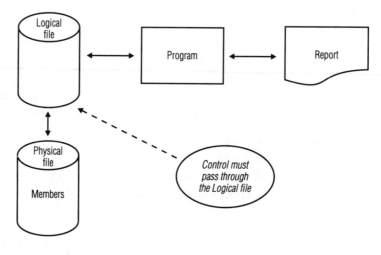

See Figure 8.3 for the **Start Source Entry Utility** screen with these changes made.

```
                        Start Source Entry Utility (STRSEU)

 Type choices, press Enter.

 Source file  . . . . . . . . . > SOURCE        Name, *PRV
   Library  . . . . . . . . . . >   YOURNAME    Name, *LIBL, *CURLIB, *PRV
 Source member  . . . . . . . .   paymstl1      Name, *PRV, *SELECT
 Source type  . . . . . . . . .   lf            Name, *SAME, BAS, BASP, C...
 Text 'description' . . . . . .   PAYMST in sequence by dept, name




                                                                        Bottom
 F3=Exit    F4=Prompt    F5=Refresh    F12=Cancel   F13=How to use this display
 F24=More keys
```

FIGURE 8.3   *Start Source Entry Utility for PAYMSTL1*

When the entries have been verified as correct,

Press	Enter

The standard SEU Edit screen will be displayed.

Press	Enter	to compress the blank lines
Type	IP	where the cursor is located
Press	Enter	

SEU will display the logical file prompt on the lower part of the screen. See Figure 8.4 for the logical file prompt.

Figure 8.5 shows the **Data Description Specification** screen. It is the same format as is used for the physical file PAYMST. A new Function parameter, PFILE, is a required entry for a logical file. The file name within the parentheses of this parameter is the link between the physical file and the logical file. The K in Name Type specifies the key fields, or fields in which the data will be sequenced. The first keyed field name listed is the major access path. The second named keyed field will be accessed next, and so on.

```
Columns . . . :   1  71            Edit              YOURNAME/SOURCE
SEU=>  _____        PAYMSTL1
FMT LF .....A..........T.Name+++++.Len++TDpB.....Functions++++++++++++++++
       *************** Beginning of data ********************************
......
       ***************** End of data ***********************************




















       Prompt type . . .  LF      Sequence number . . .  ''''''''

       Name                            Data    Decimal
       Type      Name        Length    Type    Positions    Use
       _    _____      ___       _        ___          _
       Functions
       _____

       F3=Exit   F4=Prompt   F5=Refresh       F11=Previous record
       F12=Cancel            F23=Select prompt  F24=More keys
```

FIGURE 8.4   *SEU Edit Screen with LF Prompt*

Type the Data Description Specification for PAYMSTL1, as shown in Figure 8.5.

FIGURE 8.5	***Logical File Field Information for PAYMSTL1***	
Name Type	Name	Function
R	PAYMSTR	PFILE(PAYMST)
K	DEPTNO	
K	NAME	
	EMPID	
	MONSAL	

Save the logical file description with the name of PAYMSTL1 as shown in Figure 8.6.

Press	F3	to exit and save

Compile this logical file source member.

Type	14	in the option column prior to PAYMSTL1
Press	Enter	

Check your message and output queues to ensure that the compile ended normally. If it did not, correct the errors and recompile. See Chapter 6, "Creating a Physical File Description," for further information on messages, output queue, and compiling.

```
                                    Exit

  Type choices, press Enter.

     Change/create member  . . . . . . .    Y              Y=Yes, N=No
       Member  . . . . . . . . . . . .     PAYMSTL1       Name, F4 for list
        File  . . . . . . . . . . . .      SOURCE         Name, F4 for list
          Library . . . . . . . . . . .      YOURNAME     Name
        Text  . . . . . . . . . . . .      PAYMST in sequence by dept, name

     Resequence member . . . . . . .       Y              Y=Yes, N=No
        Start . . . . . . . . . . . .      0001.00        0000.01-9999.99
        Increment . . . . . . . . . .      01.00          00.01-99.99

     Print member  . . . . . . . . .       N              Y=Yes, N=No

     Return to editing . . . . . . . .      N              Y=Yes, N=No

     Go to member list . . . . . . . .      N              Y=Yes, N=No


  F3=Exit   F4=Prompt   F5=Refresh   F12=Cancel
```

FIGURE 8.6   *SEU Exit Screen*

The PAYMSTL1 logical file can now be used by any high-level language program to access the PAYMST file, guaranteeing a keyed sequence. PAYMSTL1 can also be used by the Query/400 utility program. However, Query does not require the logical file. See Chapter 9 for information on Query.

REVIEW QUESTIONS

1. Define access path.
2. What are the two types of AS/400 access paths?
3. What are the steps to create a logical file?
4. How is the process of creating a logical file description similar to creating a physical file description?

EXERCISES

1. Enter the Data Description Specifications for a logical file that will sequence the DPTMST file into department number order. Compile this source member.
2. Enter the Data Description Specifications for a logical file that will sequence the DPTMST file into department name order. Compile this source member.
3. Enter the Data Description Specifications for a logical file that will sequence the ADRMST file into alphabetic order by city name. Compile this source member.
4. Enter the Data Description Specifications for a logical file that will sequence the ADRMST file into zip code sequence. Compile this source member.

Query/400

To understand what is required to generate a basic Query report.

To be able to create a keyed access path in Query.

INTRODUCTION		

Query/400 is an IBM-licensed program that is used to produce reports or data files from existing physical or logical files. Query can select and arrange data stored in one or more AS/400 files. Query provides an easy method to determine what data is retrieved, the format of the report, and whether the output should be printed, displayed, or stored in another file.

This chapter will provide a brief introduction to Query. For more information on Query, see the Query/400 User's Guide.

WORKING WITH THE QUERY UTILITY	A Query program will be defined to access the PAYMST physical file that was created in previous chapters.

Begin Query reporting by accessing the **Query Utility** menu.

Type	STRQRY	on any command line
Press	Enter	

Figure 9.1 shows the **Query Utilities** menu. Each of the Query options is a module that supports a different purpose.

```
QUERY                        Query Utilities
                                                    System:   XXXXXXXX
  Select one of the following:

    Query/400
        1. Work with queries
        2. Run an existing query
        3. Delete a query

    Query management
       10. Work with query management forms
       11. Work with query management queries
       12. Start a query
       13. Analyze a Query/400 definition
       14. Start a query allowing Query/400 definitions


                                                               More...
  Selection or command
  ===>_____

  F3=Exit   F4=Prompt   F9=Retrieve   F12=Cancel   F13=User support
  F16=AS/400 Mail menu
  (C) COPYRIGHT IBM CORP. 1980, 1991.
```

FIGURE 9.1   Query Utilities Menu

For this text, only option 1, Work with queries, will be utilized.

Type	1	to work with queries
Press	Enter	

Figure 9.2 shows the **Work with Queries** menu.

```
                          Work with Queries

  Type choices, press Enter.

     Option  . . . . . .  _              1=Create, 2=Change, 3=Copy, 4=Delete
                                         5=Display, 6=Print definition
                                         8=Run in batch, 9=Run
     Query . . . . . . .  _____     Name, F4 for list
       Library . . . . .      YOURNAME   Name, *LIBL, F4 for list













     F3=Exit       F4=Prompt      F5=Refresh       F12=Cancel
                                              (C) COPYRIGHT IBM CORP. 1988
```

FIGURE 9.2   Work with Queries Menu

To begin a new Query report, use the Create option.

Type	1	to create a new report
Press	Enter	

SPECIFY FILE SELECTIONS

You are now ready to specify the file that will be used by Query to generate the report.

Notice in Figure 9.3 that Query placed a 1 in the option column on the Specify file selections line. This is the only selection that is required before running a Query report.

Press	Enter	to specify a file name

Use the physical file PAYMST as the input file for Figure 9.4.

Type	PAYMST	as the file name
Press	Enter	to accept the remaining default options

```
                        Define the Query

Query . . . . . . :                   Option  . . . . . :   CREATE
  Library . . . . :      YOURNAME

Type options, press Enter.  Press F21 to select all.
  1=Select


Opt    Query Definition Option
 1     Specify file selections
 _     Define result fields
 _     Select and sequence fields
 _     Select records
 _     Select sort fields
 _     Select collating sequence
 _     Specify report column formatting
 _     Select report summary functions
 _     Define report breaks
 _     Select output type and output form
 _     Specify processing options


F3=Exit          F5=Report        F12=Cancel
F13=Layout       F18=Files        F21=Select all
```

FIGURE 9.3   Define the Query Menu

```
                      Specify File Selections

Type choices, press Enter.  Press F9 to specify an additional
  file selection.

    File . . . . . . . . .   _____     Name, F4 for list
      Library  . . . . . .   YOURNAME      Name, *LIBL, F4 for list
    Member . . . . . . . .   *FIRST        Name, *FIRST, F4 for list
    Format . . . . . . . .   *FIRST        Name, *FIRST, F4 for list














F3=Exit         F4=Prompt        F5=Report         F9=Add file
F12=Cancel      F13=Layout       F24=More keys
```

FIGURE 9.4   Specify File Selections

Query will enter PAYMSTR as the record name in the Format area. The following message will be displayed to verify the information: "Select file(s), or press Enter to confirm."

Press	Enter	after confirming that PAYMST and PAYMSTR record name are correct

Figure 9.5 shows that the system will return to the **Define the Query** menu.

```
                         Define the Query

Query . . . . . . :                    Option  . . . . . :    CREATE
   Library . . . . :        YOURNAME

Type options, press Enter.  Press F21 to select all.
  1=Select

Opt    Query Definition Option
  _    > Specify file selections
  _      Define result fields
  _      Select and sequence fields
  _      Select records
  _      Select sort fields
  _      Select collating sequence
  _      Specify report column formatting
  _      Select report summary functions
  _      Define report breaks
  _      Select output type and output form
  _      Specify processing options

F3=Exit          F5=Report
F13=Layout       F18=Files         F21=Select all
Select options, or press F3 to save or run the query.
```

FIGURE 9.5   *Define the Query with File Selected*

The 1 has been removed from the option column because the input file has been defined, A "greater than" sign (>) has been placed before the Specify file selections option. The "greater than" sign denotes that this item has been selected. As other options are selected, each will be marked with the "greater than" sign.

Specify file selections is the only required information. Note the system message at the bottom of the screen, "Select options, or press F3 to save or run the query." With the file defined, Query can now generate the report.

Press	F5	to run the report

The report has been generated in arrival sequence (the same sequence that the data was entered). Compare your work to Figure 9.6.

Note that the department numbers and employee names are not in any particular order.

Press	F12	to clear the displayed report

```
                              Display Report
                                        Report width . . . . . :      53
        Position to line  . . . . .          Shift to column  . . . . . .
        Line    ....+....1....+....2....+....3....+....4....+....5...
                EMP ID  DEPT NO  EMPLOYEE NAME      MONTHLY SALARY
        000001  1234     400     JONES, BILL           1,322.00
        000002  3567     600     SMITHE, CAROL         1,567.75
        000003  5632     200     GREEN, TOM            1,200.00
        000004  2567     100     ADAMS, MARK           1,546.50
        000005  4672     600     BLACKBERG, KAREN      1,300.00
        000006  7290     400     KLEIN, JOHN           1,400.00
        000007  1892     500     TUCKER, MARY          1,500.00
        000008  0516     400     WALKER, GARY          1,775.25
        000009  6340     100     POWERS, SUSAN         1,725.00
        000010  5718     300     HART, BOB             1,222.00
        ****** ********   End of  report   ********

                                                                 Bottom
        F3=Exit       F12=Cancel      F19=Left      F20=Right     F21=Split
```

FIGURE 9.6   *The Query Report from PAYMST*

USING AN ACCESS PATH WITH QUERY

A report is now needed from the PAYMST file in department sequence with employees listed alphabetically within each department. Resequencing the data by generating an access path requires only one additional Query option, Select sort fields. Query requires that sort fields be defined to create the access path. The PAYMST file name will remain unchanged on the Specify file selection line. To make this change, choose the sort fields menu item, as shown in Figure 9.7.

Type	1	in the option column for Select sort fields
Press	Enter	

SELECT SORT FIELDS

Fields are selected for sequencing in the Sort Priority column (see Figure 9.8). A sort priority is established on the basis of the value entered for each field. Only fields to be used for sorting have a sort priority. There are two choices for sorting each field, ascending or descending. The ascending sort places an alphabetic field in sequence from A to Z, while the descending sort is from Z to A. Numeric fields are sorted ascending from 0 to 9, while the descending sequence is from 9 to 0.

In our example, the department number is the major sort field, and the employee name is the minor sort field. This will sequence employees alphabetically within a department. Therefore a 1 will be placed in the Sort Priority column for Department Number, and a 2 will be placed in the Sort Priority column for the Name. Both fields will be sorted in ascending sequence.

```
                          Define the Query

Query . . . . . . :                  Option  . . . . . :    CREATE
  Library . . . . :      YOURNAME

Type options, press Enter.  Press F21 to select all.
  1=Select


Opt    Query Definition Option
  _   > Specify file selections
  _     Define result fields
  _     Select and sequence fields
  _     Select records
  1     Select sort fields
  _     Select collating sequence
  _     Specify report column formatting
  _     Select report summary functions
  _     Define report breaks
  _     Select output type and output form
  _     Specify processing options


F3=Exit            F5=Report
F13=Layout         F18=Files         F21=Select all
Select options, or press F3 to save or run the query.
```

FIGURE 9.7   *Define the Query Selecting Sort Fields*

On the Select Sort Fields screen, F11 is one of the available function keys. It can be used to alternate between showing just a list of the available fields and listing the fields and their text and length information.

```
                          Select Sort Fields

Type sort priority (0-999) and A (Ascending) or D (Descending) for
  the names of up to 32 fields, press Enter.

Sort
Prty A/D  Field         Text                               Len  Dec
___  _    EMPID         EMP ID                              4
1_   A    DEPTNO        DEPT NO                             3
2_   A    NAME          EMPLOYEE NAME                      20
___  _    MONSAL        MONTHLY SALARY                      6    2








                                                            Bottom
F3=Exit          F5=Report       F11=Display names only  F12=Cancel
F13=Layout       F18=Files       F20=Renumber            F24=More keys
```

FIGURE 9.8   *Select Sort Fields*

Press	F11	for the extended display of text
Press	New Line (or Tab)	to bypass the EMPID line
Type	1	in the Sort Priority column for DEPTNO
Press	Field Exit	
Type	A	in the Ascending/Descending column for DEPTNO
Type	2	in the Sort Priority column for NAME
Press	Field Exit	
Type	A	in the Ascending/Descending column for NAME

Figure 9.8 shows a screen display with this data entered.

Press	Enter

Notice the message at the bottom of the screen, "Press Enter to confirm." Notice that the fields have been resequenced into the sort priority. You must press Enter again to confirm your selections.

Press	Enter

Query can now generate the report shown in Figure 9.9 using this access path.

Press	F5	to display the report

```
                              Display Report
                                        Report width . . . . . :      53
        Position to line  . . . . .         Shift to column  . . . . . .
        Line      ....+....1....+....2....+....3....+....4....+....5...
                  DEPT NO  EMPLOYEE NAME       EMP ID  MONTHLY SALARY
        000001     100     ADAMS, MARK          2567      1,546.50
        000002     100     POWERS, SUSAN        6340      1,725.00
        000003     200     GREEN, TOM           5632      1,200.00
        000004     300     HART, BOB            5718      1,222.00
        000005     400     JONES, BILL          1234      1,322.00
        000006     400     KLEIN, JOHN          7290      1,400.00
        000007     400     WALKER, GARY         0516      1,775.25
        000008     500     TUCKER, MARY         1892      1,500.00
        000009     600     BLACKBERG, KAREN     4672      1,300.00
        000010     600     SMITHE, CAROL        3567      1,567.75
        ****** ********  End of report   ********

                                                              Bottom
        F3=Exit      F12=Cancel      F19=Left      F20=Right      F21=Split
```

FIGURE 9.9   *Query Report for Sorted PAYMST*

The Query report is generated in the requested sequence, alphabetic name within department number.

Press	F12	to return to the **Define the Query** menu

<table>
<tr><td>

**SAVE AND EXIT
QUERY**

</td><td>

Once a Query has been defined, the definition can be accessed again by saving it.

Press	F3	to access the save and exit screen

</td></tr>
</table>

The screen shown in Figure 9.10 will be displayed.

```
                           Exit this Query

     Type choices, press Enter.

        Save definition  . . .   Y            Y=Yes, N=No

        Run option . . . . . .   1            1=Run interactively
                                              2=Run in batch
                                              3=Do not run

        For a saved definition:
          Query  . . . . . . .   _____  Name
            Library  . . . . .   YOURNAME     Name, F4 for list

          Text . . . . . . . .   _____

          Authority  . . . . .   *LIBCRTAUT   *LIBCRTAUT, *CHANGE, *ALL,
                                              *EXCLUDE, *USE,
                                              authorization list name



     F4=Prompt        F5=Report       F12=Cancel        F13=Layout
     F14=Define the query
```

FIGURE 9.10   Exit this Query

Change the query to run in batch mode. The Query report will be spooled.

Press	New Line (or Tab)	to accept the Y
Type	2	as the Run option
Type	paymstq1	as the Query name
Press	Field Exit	
Press	New Line	to accept the library
Type	PAYMST Query in dept, name seq	as the Text information
Press	Enter	to save and run the Query report

The Query report will be on your output queue with the name QPQUPRFIL. The Query Exit option returns to the **Work with Queries** menu.

Press	F3	to exit the **Work with Queries** screen
Press	F3	to exit the **Query Utilities** screen

REVIEW QUESTIONS

1. What is the only mandatory definition option for Query to generate a report?
2. What is the additional needed definition for a physical file with an access path?
3. Explain the difference between ascending and descending sequences.

EXERCISES

1. Create an arrival sequence DPTMST report.
2. Create an arrival sequence ADRMST report.
3. Using Query, create a report that will sequence the DPTMST file into department number order.
4. Using Query, create a report that will sequence the DPTMST file into department name order.
5. Using Query, create a report that will sequence the ADRMST file into alphabetic order by city name.
6. Using Query, create a report that will sequence the ADRMST file into zip code sequence.
7. Refer to the Glossary for a full description of the EBCDIC collating sequence. This is a good reference for a file in which one field contains letters, special characters, and numbers—for example, product identification numbers. The sorting sequence would be different if you were to compare the AS/400 output with the same data run on a PC.

Control Language (CL) Information

To understand the necessity of a working knowledge of Control Language (CL).

To define the CL command structure.

To understand and use the CL commands that are described in detail in this chapter.

INTRODUCTION

Control Language is the operating system language on the AS/400. A working knowledge of CL is necessary for anyone who anticipates using the AS/400 on a regular basis. CL is an English-like language that has many applications on the AS/400. CL commands can be invoked from the command line and can be used as shortcuts to menus. Programs written in CL make efficient use of procedural languages, such as RPG and COBOL, and the operating system. As a programming language, CL can be used to call other programs, pass and receive parameters, call menus, and accept input from users. With a working knowledge of other procedural languages the simple structure of CL is easy to learn and use.

This chapter will introduce you to the CL command structure and many useful CL commands. There is no reference to CL programming in the chapter.

CL COMMAND STRUCTURE

Many Control Language commands were referenced in previous chapters, including WRKOBJPDM, WRKMBRPDM, STRPDM, SNDMSG, STRDFU, and WRKSPLF. The format of most CL commands is a multipart structure. Most commands include a minimum of two parts, and some commands contain three parts.

In this multipart structure, the first part of the command is the action of the command, or the verb. The last part of the command is the target of the action, or the subject. Consider the sentence "Kick the ball." Some commands have an additional middle part, which further defines the target of the action, for example, "Kick the soccer ball."

Each of these three parts of a command is one, two, or three characters. The command abbreviation is the action or target phrase, usually containing no vowels.

The first part of the command signifies the action to be taken. The following is partial list of the action or verb part of a CL command:

ABBREVIATION	DESCRIPTION
chg	change
cpy	copy
crt	create
dlt	delete
dsp	display
snd	send
str	start
wrk	work with

The second part of the command is the target of the action or, if there are three parts, a further definition of the target. The following is a partial list of the subject part of a CL command:

ABBREVIATION	DESCRIPTION
act	active
cbl	COBOL program
clp	Control Language Program
dfu	Data File Utility
f	file
job	job
lib	library
mbr	member
msg	message
obj	object
out	output
pdm	Programming Development Manager
pf	physical file
pfm	physical file member
prt	printer
pwd	password
qry	Query
rpg	Report Program Generator language
seu	Source Entry Utility
spl	spool
src	source
sys	system
usr	user
wtr	writer

Several examples of CL commands with two parts are chgpwd (change password), cpyf (copy file), and strqry (start Query).

The third part of a CL command, if it is present, is the target of the command. Therefore the second part of the command was a further definition of this target. The following is a partial list of the third part of the CL command:

ABBREVIATION	DESCRIPTION
aut	authority
d	description
f	file
job	job
pdm	Programming Development Manager
pgm	program
prf	profile
q	queue
sts	status

Several examples of CL commands with three parts are crtprtf (create printer file), dspusrprf (display user profile), and wrkobjpdm (work with objects using PDM).

Signoff, Go, and Call are examples of CL commands that are single words. On a command line, Go is used to transfer to another screen. For example, Go Main would transfer you to the **Main Menu**. Call "program name" is used to execute a program from any command line.

The end of this chapter has a list of the most common CL commands that you will use.

USING CL COMMANDS	Most AS/400 screens have a command line, and other screens have a function key that will retrieve a command line. CL commands are typed on a command line and may be prompted to receive more information about the command and the necessary parameters. If the structure of a command's parameters is known, the information can be typed directly on a command line, and the prompt can be bypassed.

You can retrieve your previously used CL commands by pressing F9. Repeated pressing of F9 will return each command that you have used during your current AS/400 session, the most recent command being retrieved first, and so on.

Some CL commands will immediately do what the command requests. For example, when STRPDM is keyed on a command line and Enter is pressed, the user will be transferred to the Start PDM menu. Other commands need more information to work and may be prompted by pressing F4. The SNDMSG command is an example of a prompted command. When SNDMSG is typed and Enter is pressed, the user receives a system message that parameters are missing.

Many CL commands have parameters to further define the command. When the command is prompted with F4, each line displayed on the command screen is a parameter with an associated default value. To obtain more information about each parameter, position the cursor on the parameter and press F4 to list all of the permitted values. The Help key will provide an explanation of each parameter value.

When changing parameter values on a CL command screen, use the Tab, New Line, or Arrow keys to bypass parameters that you do not need to change. Remember that the Field Exit key deletes characters to the right of the cursor, and Field Exit should not be used to move to the next line. If you do make a mistake, refresh the screen (F5) and start over.

Every CL command parameter consists of a keyword and a default value. If you know the parameter keyword that needs the new value, you can type that information on the command line and save a step. The standard format for using keywords is:

command keyword(value) keyword(value) . . .

You have used the WRKOUTQ command by accessing it through the **Work with Objects Using PDM** screen. This command can also be typed on any command line. WRKOUTQ must be prompted, since the parameter Output Queue needs a value. The keyword for Output Queue is OUTQ, and it needs your userid for its value.

Type	WRKOUTQ OUTQ(yourname)	on the command line
Press	Enter	

You will be transferred directly to the **Work with Output Queue** menu.

Press	F3	when you are finished looking at this screen

There is another method of using this parameter. Keywords are positional in CL. Because output queue is the first parameter, the keyword can be omitted.

Type	wrkoutq yourname	on the command line
Press	Enter	
Press	F3	when you are finished looking at this screen

To determine a command's keywords, look at a command that you have recently used. Retrieve a command on the command line with F9. This retrieval brings back the CL command and any parameters that changed. The F9 function does not show the default parameters.

Another method of determining the keywords is to press F11 when working on any command screen.

Because there are more than 850 CL commands on the AS/400, you might have problems remembering particular commands. To receive assistance in selecting the correct command,

Place	cursor	on an empty command line
Press	F4	

You will see the **Major Command Groups** menu. The commands are grouped by subject area and will allow you to more easily find the command you need.

CL commands and parameter values can be entered in lowercase and/or uppercase. The remainder of this chapter will explain specific CL commands that are useful to an operator, a user, and a programmer.

IMPORTANT CL COMMANDS

CHGPWD: Change Password
—

Your Security Officer might require you to change your password on a regular basis. Even if it is not required, you should develop the habit of changing your own password.

To change your password,

Type	CHGPWD	on a command line
Press	Enter	

See Figure 10.1.

```
                          Change Password

Password last changed . . . . . . . . . . :   02/02/92

Type choices, press Enter.

  Current password  . . . . . . . . . . .

  New password  . . . . . . . . . . . .

  New password (to verify)  . . . . . . .













 F3=Exit           F12=Cancel
```

FIGURE 10.1   *Change Password Command*

Passwords can be from one to ten characters long. As you type, the passwords will not be displayed on the **Change Password** screen. A password must begin with a letter and can contain only letters and numbers. Choose a password that you will remember but one that your friends or co-workers will not be able to guess.

Type	your existing password	for the Current password
Press	Field Exit	
Type	your new password	
Press	Field Exit	
Type	your new password	again for verification
Press	Enter	

When you sign on the next time, you will need to use the new password.

CPYF: Copy File (Print a Data File)   When changes are made to a file with DFU, a report listing only the changes is produced in your spooled output queue. However, sometimes it is necessary to have a listing of an entire data file, not just the changes. To print a physical file, the CL command CPYF must be used. Type the CPYF command on any command line, and prompt with F4. See Figure 10.2.

```
                          Copy File (CPYF)

 Type choices, press Enter.

 From file . . . . . . . . . .    _____    Name
   Library . . . . . . . . .      *LIBL         Name, *LIBL, *CURLIB
 To File . . . . . . . . . .      _____    Name, *PRINT
   Library . . . . . . . . .      *LIBL         Name, *LIBL, *CURLIB
 From member . . . . . . . .      *FIRST        Name, generic*, *FIRST, *ALL
 To member or label  . . . . .    *FIRST        Name, *FIRST, *FROMMBR
 Replace or add records  . . . .  *NONE         *NONE, *ADD, *REPLACE
 Create file . . . . . . . . .    *NO           *NO, *YES
 Print format  . . . . . . . .    *CHAR         *CHAR, *HEX




                                                                    Bottom
 F3=Exit    F4=Prompt    F5=Refresh    F10=Additional parameters   F12=Cancel
 F13=How to use this display      F24=More keys
```

FIGURE 10.2   Copy File Command

Key the name of the physical file as the From file. Key *PRINT as the To file.

Type	PAYMST	as the From file
Type	*PRINT	to send the data to a printer
Press	Enter	

A system message will flash on the bottom of your screen. The message indicates that the system is copying the file and gives the member, object, and library names. You will be returned to the screen where you entered the command, and at the bottom of the screen will be another system message specifying the number of records that were copied from the file. There will be a QSYSPRT file in your output queue that contains the list of the records from the physical file.

Display this file to verify the contents, as shown in Figure 10.3.

Compare this report with the DFU Audit Log. This report is similar to a display screen of the physical file member and provides the relative record numbers.

CRTPF: Create a Physical File

When programs output new data files, a file description must exist. A program cannot create a file description. The file description must exist before a program is executed. There are two methods for creating a file description: using Data Description Specifications and using the CRTPF (create a physical file) command.

If an external file description is necessary, a Data Description Specification should be created for the file. For a one-time application a DDS for an external file description is extra overhead and is not always needed.

```
                            Display Spooled File
 File . . . . . :   QSYSPRT                        Page/Line   1/1
 Control . . . .    _____                        Columns     1 - 78
 Find . . . . . .   _____
 *...+....1....+....2....+....3....+....4....+....5....+....6....+....7....+...
  5738SS1 VZR1M0  910524         COPY FILE              YOURNAME/PAYMST   PA
  From file . . . . . :  YOURNAME/PAYMST        Member  . . :  PAYMST
  Record length . . . :  33
  To file . . . . . . :  *PRINT
           RCDNBR  *...+... 1 ...+... 2 ...+... 3 ...+... 4 ...+... 5 ...+...
               1  1234400JONES, BILL          132200
               2  3567600SMITHE, CAROL        156775
               3  5632200GREEN, TOM           120000
               4  2567100ADAMS, MARK          154650
               5  4672600BLACKBERG, KAREN     130000
               6  7290400KLEIN, JOHN          140000
               7  1892500TUCKER, MARY         150000
               8  0516400WALKER, GARY         177525
               9  6340100POWERS, SUSAN        172500
              10  5718300HART,BOB             122200
  10 records copied to member or label *N in file QSYSPRT in library QSYS. 0 re
                                                                    More...

  F3=Exit   F12=Cancel   F19=Left   F20=Right   F24=More keys
```

FIGURE 10.3   *Display Spooled File of PAYMST CPYF Command*

Type	CRTPF	on any command line
Press	F4	to prompt

See Figure 10.4.

```
                       Create Physical File (CRTPF)

 Type choices, press Enter.

 File . . . . . . . . . . . . . .    _____       Name
   Library . . . . . . . . . .       *CURLIB          Name, *CURLIB
 Source file . . . . . . . . .       QDDSSRC          Name
   Library . . . . . . . . . .       *LIBL            Name, *LIBL, *CURLIB
 Source member . . . . . . . .       *FILE            Name, *FILE
 Record length, if no DDS . . . .    _____            Number
 Generation severity level  . . .    20               0-30
 Flagging severity level  . . . .    0                0-30
 File type . . . . . . . . . .       *DATA            *DATA, *SRC
 Member, if desired . . . . . .      *FILE            Name, *FILE, *NONE
 Text 'description' . . . . . . .    *SRCMBRTXT




                                                                   Bottom
 F3=Exit    F4=Prompt    F5=Refresh    F10=Additional parameters   F12=Cancel
 F13=How to use this display        F24=More keys
```

FIGURE 10.4   *Create Physical File Command*

The following parameters will create a record with a length of 50 characters in a physical file named CBL5OUT. The parameters and values that must be supplied are:

Type	cbl5out	as the file name
Type	50	as the record length
Type	New Master File from CBL5	as the text description
Press	F10	for additional parameters
Press	Shift/Roll Up	to the third (last) page
Type	*no	for the Record format level
Press	Enter	

A new physical file description is ready to contain data from a program.

CRTPRTF: Create a Printer File

If you are an AS/400 application programmer, there will be times when you need to have more than one print file in a procedural language program, such as COBOL or RPG. The system provides two default print files, QPRINT and QSYSPRT. QSYSPRT is often used by the operating system.

If a program has more than two print files, you must be able to create printer files when you need them. One printer file can be used by many programs and different languages. Check with your instructor for specific installation standards.

Type	CRTPRTF	on a command line
Press	F4	

See Figure 10.5.

```
                        Create Printer File (CRTPRTF)

 Type choices, press Enter.

 File . . . . . . . . . . . . .   _____    Name
   Library  . . . . . . . . . .   *CURLIB       Name, *CURLIB
 Source file  . . . . . . . . .   *NONE         Name, *NONE
   Library  . . . . . . . . . .   _____    Name, *LIBL, *CURLIB
 Source member  . . . . . . . .   *FILE         Name, *FILE
 Generation severity level  . .   20            0-30
 Flagging severity level  . . .   0             0-30
 Device specification:
   Printer  . . . . . . . . . .   *JOB          Name, *JOB, *SYSVAL
 Printer device type  . . . . .   *SCS          *SCS, *IPDS, *USERASCII
 Text 'description'  . . . . . .  *SRCMBRTXT




                                                                  Bottom
 F3=Exit   F4=Prompt   F5=Refresh   F10=Additional parameters   F12=Cancel
 F13=How to use this display    F24=More keys
```

FIGURE 10.5   Create Printer File Command

The printer file name may be up to eight characters long. The printer file name must begin with a letter and must be comprised of only letters and numbers. Key a file name and a description of the printer file. These are the only two parameters necessary.

Type	print2	as the file name
Type	Print File #2	as the description
Press	Enter	

You will now have a new *FILE object within your library named PRINT2 with an attribute of PRTF.

DSPFFD: Display File Field Description

When you need to use a physical or logical file that you did not create, you can use the DSPFFD command to obtain the field information.

Type	DSPFFD	on a command line
Press	F4	

See Figure 10.6.

```
                      Display File Field Description (DSPFFD)

 Type choices, press Enter.

 File . . . . . . . . . . . . .   _____     Name, generic*, *ALL
   Library  . . . . . . . . . .      *LIBL       Name, *LIBL, *CURLIB...
 Output . . . . . . . . . . . .   *_____       *, *PRINT, *OUTFILE

















                                                                        Bottom
 F3=Exit    F4=Prompt   F5=Refresh   F10=Additional parameters   F12=Cancel
 F13=How to use this display        F24=More keys
```

FIGURE 10.6   Display File Field Description Command

Fill in the name of the file for which you need a description, PAYMST. The asterisk in the Output parameter indicates that your display screen will be used for output. Notice that you can also direct the output to an output queue with the *PRINT parameter value.

Type	paymst	as the file name
Press	Enter	

See Figure 10.7.

```
                              Display Spooled File
File . . . . . :    QPDSPFFD                        Page/Line   1/1
Control . . . . .   _____                         Columns     1 - 78
Find . . . . . .    _____
*...+....1....+....2....+....3....+....4....+....5....+....6....+....7....+...
                           Display File Field Description
 Input parameters
    File . . . . . . . . . . . . . . . . . . . :  PAYMST
       Library . . . . . . . . . . . . . . . . :  *LIBL
 File Information
    File . . . . . . . . . . . . . . . . . . . :  PAYMST
       Library . . . . . . . . . . . . . . . . :  YOURNAME
    File location . . . . . . . . . . . . . . :  *LCL
    Externally described . . . . . . . . . . . :  Yes
    Number of record formats . . . . . . . . . :     1
    Type of file . . . . . . . . . . . . . . . :  Physical
    File creation date . . . . . . . . . . . . :  02/02/92
    Text 'description'. . . . . . . . . . . . . :  Payroll Master File Descript
 Record Format Information
    Record format . . . . . . . . . . . . . . . :  PAYMSTR
    Format level identifier . . . . . . . . . . :  278078C80EB16
                                                                     More...
 F3=Exit   F12=Cancel   F19=Left   F20=Right   F24=More keys
```

FIGURE 10.7   *Display Spooled File from DSPFFD Command*

This screen gives File and Record Format information. The File information includes file type, the creation date, and so on. The Record information includes the record format name. The next screen lists the number of fields in the record and the record length.

Press	Shift/Roll Up	to display the next screen

See Figure 10.8.

This screen shows the field names, the type of data in the field, field lengths, and the column heading information. Column heading information is duplicated and also shown as the field text.

DSPLIBL: Display Library List

This CL command displays the libraries that will be searched and the order in which they will be searched when the system is locating an object for you. When a user specifies an object name, such as the name of a file, and does not specify a library, the system searches the libraries listed until the object is found or the list is exhausted.

Type	DSPLIBL	on any command line
Press	Enter	

```
                        Display Spooled File
 File . . . . . :   QPDSPFFD              Page/Line  1/22
 Control . . . .    _____              Columns    1 - 78
 Find . . . . . .   _____
 *...+....1....+....2....+....3....+....4....+....5....+....6....+....7....+...
     Number of fields . . . . . . . . . . . . :   4
     Record length . . . . . . . . . . . . . :   33
  Field Level Information
                 Data     Field  Buffer  Buffer        Field
      Field      Type    Length  Length Position        Usage   Column Heading
      EMPID      CHAR       4       4       1           Both    EMP ID
         Field text . . . . . . . . . . . . . :  EMP ID
      DEPTNO     CHAR       3       3       5           Both    DEPT NO
         Field text . . . . . . . . . . . . . :  DEPT NO
      NAME       CHAR      20      20       8           Both    EMPLOYEE NAME
         Field text . . . . . . . . . . . . . :  EMPLOYEE NAME
      MONSAL     ZONED    6 2       6      28           Both    MONTHLY SALARY
         Field text . . . . . . . . . . . . . :  MONTHLY SALARY


                                                                    Bottom

 F3=Exit   F12=Cancel   F19=Left   F20=Right   F24=More keys
```

FIGURE 10.8   Display Spooled File from DSPFFD Command, page 2

See Figure 10.9.

```
                        Display Library List
                                              System:    XXXXXXX


 Type options, press Enter.
   5=Display objects in library

 Opt   Library     Type    Text
  _    QSYS        SYS     System Library
  _    QUSRSYS     SYS     SYSTEM LIBRARY FOR USERS
  _    QHLPSYS     SYS
  _    YOURNAME    CUR     Your Name LIBRARY
  _    QTEMP       USR
  _    YOURNAME    USR     Your Name LIBRARY
  _    QGPL        USR     GENERAL PURPOSE LIBRARY





                                                                    Bottom
 F3=Exit   F12=Cancel   F17=Top   F18=Bottom
 (C) COPYRIGHT IBM CORP. 1980, 1991.
```

FIGURE 10.9   Display Library List Command

This list represents *LIBL, which is seen as a parameter on many command screens. There are four parts to a library list, each part noted by a Type abbreviation:

system (SYS), product (PRD), current library (CUR), and user (USR). The system searches the system libraries first and subsequently the product, current, and user libraries. In Figure 10.9, yourname library appears twice, once as the current library and once as a user library. Your user library is currently active because your user profile designates your current library. The user portion of the library list is the same as the initial library list in your job description.

Your library list could be very different from this example, depending on your AS/400 environment. A product library exists when a user accesses a licensed program, for example, RPG.

DSPPFM: Display Physical File Member

You often need to look at all of the data in a physical file member. To display a physical file and the associated members,

Type	DSPPFM	on the command line
Press	F4	

See Figure 10.10.

```
                     Display Physical File Member (DSPPFM)

 Type choices, press Enter.

 File . . . . . . . . . . . . .    _____     Name
   Library  . . . . . . . . . .       *LIBL       Name, *LIBL, *CURLIB
 Member . . . . . . . . . . . .      *FIRST       Name, *FIRST, *LAST
 From record  . . . . . . . . .         1         Number, *END













                                                                     Bottom
 F3=Exit    F4=Prompt   F5=Refresh   F12=Cancel   F13=How to use this display
 F24=More keys
```

FIGURE 10.10   Display Physical File Member Command

Type	PAYMST	as the file name
Press	Enter	

Figure 10.11 should look familiar. It is same screen that is displayed from the **Work with Members Using PDM** menu.

```
                        Display Physical File Member
   File . . . . . . :    PAYMST         Library . . . . :   YOURNAME
   Member . . . . . :    PAYMST         Record . . . . . :   1
   Control . . . . :                    Column . . . . . :   1
   Find . . . . . . :
   *...+....1....+....2....+....3...
   1234400JONES, BILL             132200
   3567600SMITHE, CAROL           156775
   5632200GREEN, TOM              120000
   2567100ADAMS, MARK             154650
   4672600BLACKBERG, KAREN        130000
   7290400KLEIN, JOHN             140000
   1892500TUCKER, MARY            150000
   0516400WALKER, GARY            177525
   6340100POWERS, SUSAN           172500
   5718300HART, BOB               122200
                        ****** END OF DATA ******




                                                                      Bottom
   F3=Exit    F12=Cancel    F19=Left    F20=Right    F24=More keys
```

FIGURE 10.11   Display Physical File Member of PAYMST

**DSPUSRPRF:
Display User Profile**

All users of the AS/400 must have a user profile containing the user's authority on the system. The user profile tells the system who can sign on and what functions each user can perform after signing on.

A user profile contains the userid (the user's sign-on name), the user's password, the user library name, initial menu, job description name, output queue name, message queue name, and so on. The user profile controls a user's access to objects outside his or her library on the system. To view your own user profile,

Type	DSPUSRPRF	on a command line
Press	F4	

See Figure 10.12

Type	your userid	for the user profile name
Press	Enter	

See Figure 10.13.

This is the first of three screens of information about your user profile. Your parameter values may vary from those shown here, depending on your AS/400 security level and environment. Read your user profile, using the Help key for more information about each parameter.

```
                      Display User Profile (DSPUSRPRF)

 Type choices, press Enter.

 User profile . . . . . . . . . .   _____     Name, generic*, *ALL
 Type of information  . . . . . .   *BASIC         *BASIC, *ALL, *CMDAUT...
 Output . . . . . . . . . . . .    *_____      *, *PRINT, *OUTFILE




















                                                                  Bottom
 F3=Exit    F4=Prompt    F5=Refresh    F12=Cancel   F13=How to use this display
 F24=More keys
```

FIGURE 10.12   Display User Profile Command

```
                      Display User Profile - Basic

 User profile . . . . . . . . . . . . . . :   YOURNAME

 Previous sign-on . . . . . . . . . . . . :   02/02/92  12:46:08
 Sign-on attempts not valid . . . . . . . :   0
 Status . . . . . . . . . . . . . . . . . :   *ENABLED
 Date password last changed . . . . . . . :   02/02/92
 Password expiration interval . . . . . . :   *SYSVAL
 Set password to expired  . . . . . . . . :   *NO
 User class . . . . . . . . . . . . . . . :   *PGMR
 Special authority  . . . . . . . . . . . :   *NONE
 Group profile  . . . . . . . . . . . . . :   STUDENT
 Owner  . . . . . . . . . . . . . . . . . :   *USRPRF
 Group authority  . . . . . . . . . . . . :   *NONE
 Assistance level . . . . . . . . . . . . :   *SYSVAL
 Current library  . . . . . . . . . . . . :   YOURNAME
 Initial menu . . . . . . . . . . . . . . :   MAIN
    Library  . . . . . . . . . . . . . . . :    *LIBL
                                                              More...
 Press Enter to continue.

 F3=Exit   F12=Cancel
 (C) COPYRIGHT IBM CORP. 1980, 1991.
```

FIGURE 10.13   Display a User's Profile with Parameters

COMMON CL COMMANDS

The following list is a summary of CL commands that are commonly utilized.

COMMAND	DESCRIPTION
chgpwd	change password
cpyf	copy a file
crtcblpgm	create a COBOL/400 program
crtclppgm	create a Control Language Program program
crtpf	create a physical file
crtprtf	create a printer file
crtrpgpgm	create an RPG/400 program
dspffd	display a file's field descriptions
dspjobd	display a job description
dspmsg	display messages (same as wrkmsg)
dsppfm	display a physical file member
dspusrprf	display a user profile
runqry	run a query program
strdfu	start Data File Utility
strpdm	start Programming Development Manager
strseu	start Source Entry Utility
wrkactjob	work with active jobs
wrkmbrpdm	work with members using Programming Development Manager
wrkmsg	work with messages (same as dspmsg)
wrkobjpdm	work with objects using Programming Development Manager
wrkoutq	work with output queue
wrksplf	work with spool file
wrksyssts	work with system status
wrkusrprf	work with user profile

REVIEW QUESTIONS

1. Explain the use of Control Language (CL) on the AS/400.

2. Explain the three-part CL command structure. Define crt, wrk, q, and f.

3. Give two examples of CL commands with two parts and three examples of CL commands with three parts, using commands from the list of common CL commands.

4. What occurs when a CL command is prompted?

EXERCISES

1. Use the CPYF command to print ADRMST and DPTMST, the files created in Chapters 5 and 6.

2. Use the DSPFFD command to display the data in ADRMST. Compare this screen to the output from Exercise 1. How do they differ?

3. Print your user profile, sending the output to the printer. What command and keywords were necessary? Save this for reference.

Keyboard Usage

DISPLAY STATION KEYBOARD FUNCTION KEYS

There are two kinds of function keys on a keyboard: numbered function keys and named function keys. The display station has 24 numbered function keys.

The named function keys have words, abbreviations of words, or symbols printed on them instead of numbers. These keys usually perform the functions that the words or symbols indicate. The following list gives a brief explanation of the named function keys that you will be using most often, which are different from those on the PC keyboard. For an explanation of every key, refer to an IBM AS/400 manual (New User's Guide or a display station user's guide).

SHIFT LOCK KEY

There is no Caps Lock key.

The Shift Lock key (looks like a padlock) puts the entire keyboard in uppercase. The number keys are also changed. The Caps Lock key is not a toggle key. It will not reset the keyboard to lowercase (as on a PC keyboard) if you press it. You must press Shift/Reset.

ENTER KEY

The Enter key works as usual. However, the numeric keypad Field Plus key is not an Enter key.

FIELD EXIT KEY

The Field Exit key moves the cursor to the next field, but any characters at and to the right of the cursor in the field where you were typing are deleted. Therefore DO NOT USE THIS KEY TO MOVE FROM A FILLED FIELD TO ANOTHER FIELD! Use the New Line key or the Tab key for this movement.

FIELD PLUS AND MINUS KEYS

The Field Plus and Minus keys vary by keyboard and by system. See the Display Station User Guide for additional information.

HELP KEY

The Help key activates the AS/400 online Help.

NEW LINE KEY

The New Line key moves the cursor to the next input field in the next line. It is located in the group of named function keys between the standard keyboard and the numeric keypad. It is the bent left arrow key to the left of the Insert key.

PRINT KEY

The Print key sends a copy of the current display screen to the output queue, and this copy can be sent to the printer at a later time. A message will be shown that this has occurred, and the keyboard will be locked. You will need to press the Reset key to unlock the keyboard.

RESET KEY

The Reset key is used to correct or reset a keyboard error. You can often lock the keyboard by pressing a wrong key, or certain messages will lock the keyboard. Press this key to unlock the keyboard.

SHIFT/ROLL KEYS

The combination Shift/Up Arrow keys (Shift/Roll Up) cause a display that has "More..." or "+" on the lower right edge of the screen to show the next screen of data. The combination Shift/Down Arrow keys (Shift/Roll Down) cause the previous screen to be displayed.

PC KEYBOARD FUNCTION KEYS

This appendix assumes that PC Support is being used with the standard default keyboard mapping when connecting an IBM PS/2 to the AS/400 with twinaxial cable. If your installation utilizes another type of connection, this appendix might not be helpful.

There are two kinds of function keys on a keyboard: numbered function keys and named function keys. The PC has only 12 function keys. To use the F13 through F24 keys on a PC, press and hold the Shift key and press the function key that, when added to 12, will result in the correct key. For example, Shift/F1 is used for F13, Shift/F8 is used for F20.

The named function keys have words, abbreviations of words, or symbols printed on them instead of numbers. These keys usually perform the functions that the words or symbols indicate. However, if you are using a PC keyboard, these PC named function keys take on new meanings. The following list gives a brief explanation of the named function keys that you will be using most often that have different meanings or functions than the typical PC keyboard. For an explanation of every key, refer to an IBM AS/400 manual (New User's Guide or a display station user's guide).

CAPS LOCK KEY

The Caps Lock key puts only the alphabetic keys in uppercase. It is a toggle key and will reset the keyboard to lowercase when pressed.

There is no Shift Lock key.

ENTER KEY

The Enter key works as usual. However, it is in a different position on this keyboard than on the display station keyboard. Be careful if you switch between keyboards!

FIELD EXIT KEY

The Field Exit key is the right Ctrl key. It moves the cursor to the next field, but any characters at and to the right of the cursor in the field where you were typing are deleted. Therefore DO NOT USE THIS KEY TO MOVE FROM A FILLED FIELD TO ANOTHER FIELD! Use the New Line key or the Tab key for this movement.

FIELD PLUS AND MINUS KEYS

The Field Plus and Minus keys vary by keyboard and by system. See the keyboard mapping information for your installation.

HELP KEY

The Help key is the F1 or Scroll Lock (Break) key.

NEW LINE KEY

The New Line key is the combination Shift/Enter keys. BE CAREFUL to press and hold the Shift and then press the Enter key! This combination of keys moves the cursor to the next input field in the next line.

PRINT KEY

The Print key is the combination Shift/Print Screen keys. Hold the Shift key and press the Print Screen key. This sends a copy of the current display screen to the output queue. A message will be shown that this has occurred, and the keyboard will be locked. You will need to press the Reset key (left Ctrl key) to unlock the keyboard.

RESET KEY

The Reset key is the lower left Ctrl key. It is used to correct or reset a keyboard error.

PAGE UP/DOWN (SHIFT/ROLL) KEYS

The Shift/Roll Up occurs with the Page Down key. The Shift/Roll Down occurs with the Page Up key. These keys cause a display that has "More..." or "+" on the lower right edge of the screen to show the next (or previous) screen of data.

SEU
Information

OVERVIEW OF SEU EDITING INFORMATION

To move the cursor to text that is not currently displayed on the screen, use the Shift/Roll Up or Shift/Roll Down keys.

CHANGE LINES

Use the Arrow keys to position the cursor where changes need to be made. Use the Insert and Delete keys as you would with a word processor.

Type a P in the sequence number to display the line in prompt mode. Press F4 anywhere within the line to have the line prompted.

COPY

See Other Useful Line Commands

DELETE LINE

Place a D in the sequence number and press Enter.

FREE FORM LINE ADDITIONS OR CHANGES

Press F12 to leave the prompt portion and use the Arrow keys to move around the screen text and correct typing errors.

HELP

Place the cursor in the sequence number and press the Help key. On a prompted line, the Help key will give information about the content of the field where the cursor is located.

INSERT LINES

Place an I in the sequence number of the line and press Enter. A new line will be inserted *after* the sequence number.

Place an IP in the sequence number if you want to receive a prompt and the new line will be the same type as the current line.

The prompt can be changed by pressing F23 and selecting a new prompt type from the menu.

MOVE

See Other Useful Line Commands

OTHER USEFUL LINE COMMANDS

These commands must be typed over the sequence number.

ABBREVIATION	DESCRIPTION
A	copy or move the specified line(s), marked by C, CC, M, or MM, *after* this line
B	copy or move the specified line(s), marked by C, CC, M, or MM, *before* this line
C	copy this line to target line specified by A or B
CC	copy this block of lines (defined by a pair of CC commands) to the target specified by A or B
COLS	enters a line with column numbers on the line above the current line
DD	delete this block of lines (defined by a pair of DD commands)
L	shift the data in this line one character position to the left
M	move this line to target line specified by A or B
MM	move this block of lines (defined by a pair of MM commands) to the target specified by A or B
R	shift the data in this line one character position to the right
RP	repeat this line once, immediately below this line
RPx	repeat this line x number of times immediately below this line
RPP	repeat this block of lines (defined by a pair of RPP commands) immediately below this marked block

SEU COMMAND LINE INFORMATION

Enter the following SEU commands on the SEU command line at the top of the screen (F10 places the cursor on this command line).

SEU COMMAND	DESCRIPTION
SAVE	save a file without exiting the current SEU session
CANCEL or CAN	cancel this SEU session and return to the previous menu
CHANGE or C	change a string of characters
FIND or F	search for a string of characters
TOP or T	move to the top of the source member
BOTTOM or B	move to the bottom of the source member

Use the Help key to learn more about the SEU options.

FUNCTION KEYS

FUNCTION KEY	DESCRIPTION
F4 = Prompt	This key places the line that the cursor is on in a prompt.
F10 = Cursor	Press F10 to move the cursor from the data area to the command line or from the command line to the data area.
F11 = Previous Record	This key places the previous line in a prompt. The Prompt mode must be active. The Enter key places the next line in a prompt.
F13 = Change session defaults	This option allows you to change the manner in which you work with SEU. The defaults include the amount the screen rolls when Shift/Roll Up or Shift/Roll Down is pressed, uppercase input only, and syntax checking.
F15 = Browse/Copy options	This option splits the screen in half horizontally, leaving the source member in the top portion and placing the most recent compiler output of this member in the bottom portion. (See Appendix C for more information on split-screen editing.) This gives you the ability to look at the error messages and correct the source code at the same time. The cursor can be moved from the upper to the lower half with the Arrow keys.

FUNCTION KEY	DESCRIPTION
F21 = System command	This key displays a window in which you can enter CL commands.
F23 = Select prompt	Press F23 to display all possible prompt formats, and you will see Figure B.1 for the **Select Prompt** menu.

```
                        Select Prompt

  Type choice, press Enter.

   Prompt type . . . . . . . . . . .  __       Values listed below

     RPG/400:        H,F,FC,FK,FX,U,E,L,I,IX,J (I cont),JX,DS,SS,SV,C,O,
                     OD,P (O cont),N,* (Comment)
     COBOL:          CB,C*
     REFORMAT/SORT:  RH,RR,RF,RC
     DDS:            LF (Logical file),PF (Physical file),
                     BC (Interactive Communications Feature file),
                     DP (Display and Printer file),
                     A* (Comment)
     MNU:            MS,MH,MD,MC (MD cont),CC (Comment)
     FORTRAN:        FT, F*
     Other:          NC (No syntax checking),** (Free format)




  F12=Cancel    F23=Select user prompt
```

FIGURE B.1   Select Prompt

SEU has stored 40 formats for use in programming languages or utility programs. Choose the appropriate format or use free format.

APPENDIX · C

Entering
and Compiling
Source Members

The Source Entry Utility (SEU) will be used to enter source member code for any programming language on the AS/400. These program instructions will be entered as members within an object PF-SRC. After the instructions have been entered, the instructions will need to be compiled. A compiler checks for syntax errors and generates an executable object if there are no syntax errors. Syntax errors are errors in the language—misspelled reserved words or variable names, entries in the wrong columns, and so forth. Only after the instructions are syntax error free will the AS/400 produce an executable object that can be run.

To compile any source member, begin on the **Work With Members Using PDM** screen and enter option 14 (to compile) before the member name. A system informational message will inform you whether your compile ended normally or abnormally. The output of the compile is a listing of the instruction code and any errors. This can be reviewed by displaying the spooled output file, which will be in your output queue.

If there are syntax errors, they must be corrected by editing the member in SEU. After the corrections are made, the member is again compiled. A "clean compile" produces a new object with the same name as the member. The new object will have a type of *PGM, and an attribute of the instruction code—for example, CBL for COBOL, CLP for Control Language Program, RPG for RPG/400, and so on. This object can then be run (executed) with option 16 on the **Work with Objects Using PDM** screen or with the CL command CALL. Running (or executing) an object will show any logic errors and, if the object is error free, produce the expected output.

The following sections will give instructions for entering any source code. The instructions for using SEU are in Appendix B.

ENTERING SOURCE MEMBERS

Access the **Work with Objects Using PDM** screen. All of your application source code members will be held as members within the source physical file object named SOURCE. To place members within this file, you must first "Work with" the SOURCE file.

Type	wrkobjpdm	on any command line
Press	Enter	
Type	12	in the option column for SOURCE
Press	Enter	

The screen should show the **Work with Members Using PDM** screen. Remember that you are now inside the SOURCE file and will be creating members within this source physical file.

T I P   **You may type WRKMBRPDM on any command line to quickly access this screen.**

To create a new source member, the Create command must be invoked. This command will create a new member and automatically transfer to SEU.

Press	F6	to create a new member

The **Start Source Entry Utility** screen will be displayed, as shown in Figure C.1.

```
                        Start Source Entry Utility (STRSEU)

 Type choices, press Enter.

 Source file  . . . . . . . . . > SOURCE        Name, *PRV
   Library  . . . . . . . . . . >   YOURNAME    Name, *LIBL, *CURLIB, *PRV
 Source member  . . . . . . . .   *PRV          Name, *PRV, *SELECT
 Source type  . . . . . . . . .   *SAME         Name, *SAME, BAS, BASP, C...
 Text 'description'  . . . . . .  *BLANK_____




















                                                                        Bottom
 F3=Exit   F4=Prompt   F5=Refresh   F12=Cancel   F13=How to use this display
 F24=More keys
```

FIGURE C.1   Start Source Entry Utility

The five entries from this screen will be used by the Create function to place the source code member within your library and within the SOURCE file. Type the source member name, source type (CBL, RPG, CLP, and so on), and description entries, pressing Field Exit after each item. The description entry is not necessary, but you should type a descriptive comment about the source code. Press Enter only when all the entries are typed and are correct.

The SEU entry screen is now displayed. The top right portion of the screen lists the library and source file that hold this particular source member. Immediately below, on the next line, the source code name is displayed. The center of the screen will hold the source code program instructions. The lower part of the screen lists the function keys that may be used in SEU. The very bottom line should have a message that the member has been added to the SOURCE file. See Figure C.2 to verify that the Create function completed normally.

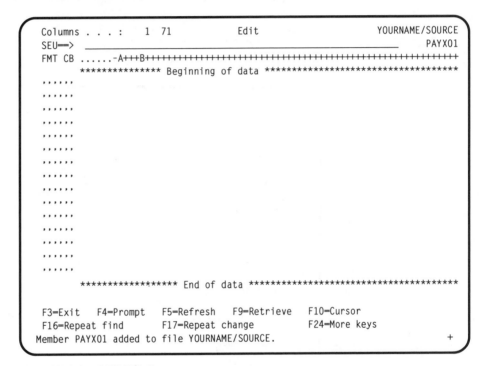

```
 Columns . . . :    1  71              Edit              YOURNAME/SOURCE
 SEU==>  _____           PAYX01
 FMT CB ......-A+++B+++++++++++++++++++++++++++++++++++++++++++++++++++++++
         *************** Beginning of data ********************************
 ,,,,,,
 ,,,,,,
 ,,,,,,
 ,,,,,,
 ,,,,,,
 ,,,,,,
 ,,,,,,
 ,,,,,,
 ,,,,,,
 ,,,,,,
 ,,,,,,
 ,,,,,,
 ,,,,,,
 ,,,,,,
         ***************** End of data **********************************

 F3=Exit   F4=Prompt   F5=Refresh   F9=Retrieve   F10=Cursor
 F16=Repeat find       F17=Repeat change          F24=More keys
 Member PAYX01 added to file YOURNAME/SOURCE.                          +
```

FIGURE C.2   SEU Edit Screen

Figure C.2 is an example of a COBOL source code screen. Depending on the source member type, this will differ. SEU chooses which form to present based on the source type you defined on the **Start Source Entry Utility** screen. If you are keying in CL source code, you will want to type in a command and then press F4. SEU will then give you the correct parameters for the particular CL command.

For all other languages, use these instructions:

Press	Enter	to compress and position the cursor
Type	IP	in the Beginning of data line
Press	Enter	

The I stands for "Insert data lines," and the P requests that the source code member be entered using predefined prompts. The AS/400 will automatically display the correct source code prompt on the lower portion of the screen.

While you are entering any source member code, you can save the code at any time.

Type	SAVE	on the SEU command line
Press	Enter	

The Save command is considerably faster than pressing F3 and changing the Return to editing to Yes.

When you have completed entering the source code,

Press	F3	to exit and save your work

The **Exit** screen is shown in Figure C.3.

```
                                  Exit

   Type choices, press Enter.

      Change/create member  . . . . . . .    Y           Y=Yes, N=No
        Member  . . . . . . . . . . . . .    PAYX01      Name, F4 for list
        File  . . . . . . . . . . . . . .    SOURCE      Name, F4 for list
          Library . . . . . . . . . . . .    YOURNAME    Name
        Text  . . . . . . . . . . . . . .    Payroll Master File Report

      Resequence member . . . . . . . .      Y           Y=Yes, N=No
        Start . . . . . . . . . . . . .      0001.00     0000.01-9999.99
        Increment . . . . . . . . . . .      01.00       00.01-99.99

      Print member  . . . . . . . . . .      N           Y=Yes, N=No

      Return to editing . . . . . . . .      N           Y=Yes, N=No

      Go to member list . . . . . . . .      N           Y=Yes, N=No



   F3=Exit    F4=Prompt    F5=Refresh    F12=Cancel
```

FIGURE C.3   SEU Exit Screen

These options can be changed, but this is not necessary. Note that this is the same screen that was seen after entering the physical file description for the Payroll Master File in Chapter 6.

Press	Enter	to accept the default options

You will return to the **Work with Members Using PDM** screen, and your new source code member will be listed, with its type and description.

COMPILING A SOURCE CODE MEMBER

You are now ready to compile the source code member. Use the F23 function key to display more options. You will see the option to compile a member.

Press	F23	to display more options
Type	14	in the appropriate Options (Opt) column
Press	Enter	

Remember that compiles are batch jobs. You can do other things while you are waiting for the compile job to finish.

When the compile is completed, you will receive a system information message. View your messages.

Type	dm	on the option line to determine whether the compile completed normally with no syntax errors or abnormally
Press	Enter	

If the source code member did not compile correctly, display the compile listing.

Type	sp	to access the output queue to find the errors

You may need to print the compiler output until you become proficient in working with your source language. The syntax error messages are printed either after the source line that is in error or at the end of the source code with line number references to the source statements in error.

Verify your syntax, use SEU to correct the mistakes, and compile the program again.

SPLIT-SCREEN EDITING

Split-screen editing is a helpful method for editing your source member. You can edit and view your compiler output at the same time. Use the edit option to access the source file member. Once you are in SEU, F15 will initiate the split-screen process.

Type	2	to edit the member
Press	F15	for split-screen editing

You will see the **Browse/Copy Options** screen shown in Figure C.4.

Type	2	in Selection to copy a spool file to the screen
Press	Enter	

You will return to the SEU Edit mode, and the screen will be split horizontally. The member that you are editing will be on the upper half of the screen, and the most recent compiler output will be on the lower half of your screen. This gives you the ability to look at the error messages and correct the source code at the same time. The cursor can be moved from the upper to the lower half with the Arrow keys. The F12 key will return the screen to full Edit mode.

```
                          Browse/Copy Options

  Type choices, press Enter.

    Selection . . . . . . . . . .   1              1=Member
                                                   2=Spool file
                                                   3=Output queue
    Copy all records  . . . . . .   N              Y=Yes, N=No
    Browse/copy member  . . . . .   PAYX01         Name, F4 for list
      File  . . . . . . . . . . .     SOURCE       Name, F4 for list
        Library . . . . . . . . .     YOURNAME     Name, *CURLIB, *LIBL

    Browse/copy spool file  . . .   PAYX01         Name, F4 for list
      Job . . . . . . . . . . . .     PAYX01       Name
        User  . . . . . . . . . .       YOURNAME   Name, F4 for list
        Job number  . . . . . . .         *LAST    Number, *LAST
        Spool number  . . . . . .         *LAST    Number, *LAST, *ONLY

    Display output queue  . . . .   QPRINT         Name, *ALL
      Library . . . . . . . . . .     *LIBL        Name, *CURLIB, *LIBL

  F3=Exit        F4=Prompt      F5=Refresh        F12=Cancel
  F13=Change session defaults   F14=Find/Change options
```

FIGURE C.4   Browse/Copy Options

An easy method to locate your syntax errors is to use the Find command on the SEU command line of the spool file. The error messages can be found by looking for *ERR. Using these two items together will take you to the first error message. Depending on the language, the syntax error messages may be embedded in the source code itself (for example, CL) or be at the end of the source code (for example, COBOL). RPG has error messages at the end but flags the source code line with the error message number.

Position	cursor	on the SEU command line
Type	F *ERR	F to find, *ERR for error messages
Press	Enter	to locate first error message
Press	F16	to repeat this process and find the next error. Repeat for additional syntax errors.

COMPILED OBJECTS

When the source code member has compiled correctly, an executable object will be created and placed within your library. Any entry with the *PGM type is an executable or machine language object and cannot be placed within SOURCE. Therefore the *PGM object can be found only on the **Work with Objects Using PDM** screen.

Return to the **Work with Objects Using PDM** screen and verify that the executable object has been created. Accessing the **Work with Objects Using PDM** screen depends on the method you used to access the **Work with Members Using PDM** screen.

If you accessed the **Work with Members Using PDM** screen by working with SOURCE on the **Work with Objects Using PDM** screen,

Press	F12	to return to the **Work with Objects Using PDM** screen

Or if you used the CL command WRKMBRPDM, the F12 key will return you to the screen where you entered that command. Therefore

Type	wrkobjpdm	on a command line

Once the **Work with Objects Using PDM** screen is displayed, refresh the screen to ensure that all the objects are displayed.

Press	F5	

You will see a new object listed that has the same name as the SOURCE member. This object has a type of *PGM and an attribute of the source language. Any entry with the *PGM type is an executable or machine language object.

T I P

These objects may be executed (or run) by typing a 16 in the Opt column. You can also execute (run) any program from any command line by entering CALL "program name" and pressing Enter.

SUMMARY

1. Create and enter the source code using SEU (Source Entry Utility).

2. Compile the source code, using option 14 on your SOURCE member. You always receive a message for a normal or abnormal compile.

3. If the source member compiles correctly, you will have created a *PGM object in your library with an attribute of the source member. The output listing (found in your output queue) will contain no fatal error messages.

4. To correct language instruction code errors, edit the source member using SEU. Remember to use the split-screen option. If there are too many errors to correct on the screen, you can print the compiler output. When the source member has been corrected, compile the member again.

5. When a source member is recompiled after its executable object already exists, a **Confirm Compile of Member** screen appears when you initiate a compile. You have the option to delete the existing object for this member. You must respond Y, for yes, if you want to create a new (and hopefully correct) executable object.

   If you press Enter, the default is no. You will have changed your source code but not changed the executable object code, since the source member will not be recompiled.

6. When you have created a *PGM, either run that executable code with option 16 from the **Work with Objects Using PDM** screen or stay on the **Work with Members Using PDM** screen and enter Call "program name" on the command line.

T I P

If you want only a copy of your source code without the compiler information, use option 6 on the Work with Members Using PDM screen. Print the listing as usual through your output queue. The file name of this spooled file is QPSUPRTF.

A Sample COBOL Program

INTRODUCTION

The following sections give instructions for entering and compiling COBOL source code. The program will list the Payroll Master File that was created in Chapters 6 and 7. Remember that the instructions for using SEU are in Appendix B, and more information on entering and compiling source members is in Appendix C.

ENTERING A COBOL SOURCE MEMBER

COBOL/400 instructions will now be entered for a program to print the Payroll Master File (PAYMST) data. The COBOL source member name will be PAYB01. This name is derived from the following abbreviations:

PAY (PAYMST file)
B (a COBOL program)
01 (the first COBOL program for the PAYMST file)

Access the **Work with Members Using PDM** screen. You need to create a COBOL source member. F6 is the Create command. This command will create a member and transfer you to SEU.

Press	F6	to create the new COBOL member

The **Start Source Entry Utility** screen will be displayed on the screen.

The five entries on the screen are required by the Create function to place the program within your library and within the SOURCE file. The program will have a type of CBL (for COBOL) and a program description.

Type	PAYB01	for the source member name
Press	Field Exit	
Type	CBL	for the source type
Press	Field Exit	
Type	Payroll Master File Report	for the description

Compare the entries with Figure D.1. When all of the entries are as shown,

Press	Enter

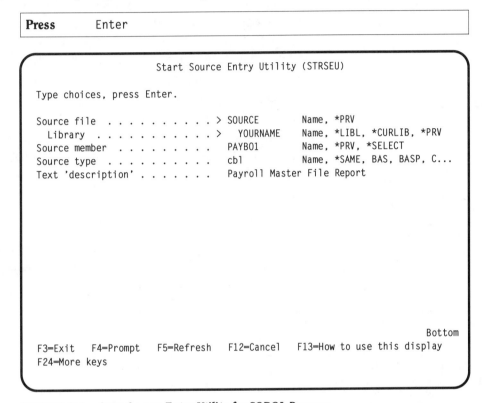

```
                    Start Source Entry Utility (STRSEU)

 Type choices, press Enter.

 Source file  . . . . . . . . . > SOURCE        Name, *PRV
   Library  . . . . . . . . . . >  YOURNAME     Name, *LIBL, *CURLIB, *PRV
 Source member  . . . . . . . .   PAYB01        Name, *PRV, *SELECT
 Source type  . . . . . . . . .   cbl           Name, *SAME, BAS, BASP, C...
 Text 'description' . . . . . .   Payroll Master File Report







                                                                     Bottom
 F3=Exit   F4=Prompt   F5=Refresh   F12=Cancel   F13=How to use this display
 F24=More keys
```

FIGURE D.1   *Start Source Entry Utility for COBOL Program*

The SEU Edit screen is now displayed.

Press	Enter	to compress blank lines and position the cursor
Type	IP	in the sequence number area of the Beginning of data line
Press	Enter	

The AS/400 will automatically display the COBOL prompt, CB, on the lower portion of the screen. This COBOL prompt contains three parts: Continuation, Area-A, and Area-B. If you do not need to use Continuation or Area-A, use the Field Exit key to bypass these. All keying will appear in uppercase. When you type "PROCEDURE DIVISION," you will need to start in AREA-A and keep typing into AREA-B. When you have completed a line of code, press Enter, and that line will be moved to the top of the screen with a blank prompt at the bottom.

The Tab key in SEU does not function as you might expect. To align Pictures, you must use the spacebar. Watch the column numbers shown on the screen so that you can be consistent. You can also type COLS in the sequence number area, and a line with column numbers will appear above the current line. This line can be deleted by typing a D in the sequence number area.

You will be keying the program as shown in Figure D.2. Be sure to change all of the occurrences of YOURNAME to your userid. There are two items in this program that are specific to COBOL/400. The input file name in the SELECT statement is DISK-PAYMST. As the file is being read sequentially, the file is assigned to disk (database would be required if the access were keyed). PAYMST is the name of the physical file member that is being read from your library.

The COPY statement is used to retrieve COBOL source code into an existing source member. The use of COPY for record formats ensures that the correct field and record length are used. COBOL/400 can retrieve a physical or logical file description that was created by using Data Description Specifications (DDS). Note in the WORKING-STORAGE SECTION that MASTER-IN is a COBOL COPY of the physical file description created in Chapter 6. The format of this COPY statement is unique to the AS/400:

COPY DDS-PAYMSTR OF YOURNAME-PAYMST

Following "DDS-" is the record name, PAYMSTR, of the physical file. Your library name replaces YOURNAME. PAYMST is the name of the physical file in your library.

FIGURE D.2   ***COBOL Program***

COBOL CODING FORM

```
01  IDENTIFICATION DIVISION.
02  PROGRAM-ID. PAYB01.
03  AUTHOR. YOURNAME.
04  DATE-WRITTEN. 12/19/91.
05 ***  THIS PROGRAM WILL READ THE PAYROLL MASTER FILE
06 ***  AND PRINT A LIST OF THE FILE CONTENTS.
07  ENVIRONMENT DIVISION.
08  CONFIGURATION SECTION.
09  SOURCE-COMPUTER. IBM-AS400.
10  OBJECT-COMPUTER. IBM-AS400.
11  INPUT-OUTPUT SECTION.
12  FILE-CONTROL.
13      SELECT PAY-MASTER-FILE ASSIGN TO DISK-PAYMST.
14      SELECT REPORT-OUT     ASSIGN TO PRINTER-QPRINT.
15  DATA DIVISION.
16  FILE SECTION.
17  FD  PAY-MASTER-FILE       LABEL RECORDS ARE STANDARD.
18  01  PAY-MASTER-RECORD      PIC X(40).
19  FD  REPORT-OUT            LABEL RECORDS ARE OMITTED.
20  01  REPORT-RECORD          PIC X(132).
```

FIGURE D.2   **COBOL Program continued**

COBOL CODING FORM

PROGRAM		REQUESTED BY		PAGE 2 OF 5
PROGRAMMER		DATE		IDENT. 73 80

```
01   WORKING-STORAGE SECTION.
02   01   WORK-AREAS.
03        05   MORE-RECORDS         PIC X(3)  VALUE "YES".
04        05   LINE-COUNT           PIC 9(2)  VALUE ZERO.
05        05   PAGE-COUNT           PIC 9(3)  VALUE ZERO.
06        05   RUN-DATE
07             10   YY               PIC X(2).
08             10   MM               PIC X(2).
09             10   DD               PIC X(2).
10   01   MASTER-IN.
11        COPY DDS-PAYMSTR OF YOURNAME-PAYMST.
12   01   HEADER-1.
13        05   FILLER               PIC X(40)  VALUE "YOURNAME".
14        05   FILLER               PIC X(92)  VALUE "COBOL SECTION 1".
15   01   HEADER-2.
16        05   HEADER-DATE          PIC X(8).
17        05   FILLER               PIC X(11)  VALUE SPACE.
18        05   FILLER               PIC X(27)  VALUE "PAYROLL REPORT".
19        05   FILLER               PIC X(5)   VALUE "PAGE".
20        05   PAGE-NUMBER          PIC Z(3).
          05   FILLER               PIC X(78)  VALUE SPACE.
     01   HEADER-3.
          05   FILLER               PIC X(24)  VALUE "EMPLOYEE NAME".
          05   FILLER               PIC X(108)  VALUE
               "EMP ID   DEPT NO     HON SAL".
```

COBOL CODING FORM

PROGRAM		REQUESTED BY		PAGE 3 OF 5
PROGRAMMER		DATE		IDENT. 73 80

```
01   01   DETAIL-LINE.
02        05   DL-NAME              PIC X(20).
03        05   FILLER               PIC X(5).
04        05   DL-EMPID             PIC X(4).
05        05   FILLER               PIC X(6).
06        05   DL-DEPTNO            PIC X(3).
07        05   FILLER               PIC X(6).
08        05   DL-MONSAL            PIC Z,ZZZ.99.
09        05   FILLER               PIC X(78).
10   PROCEDURE DIVISION.
11   100-MAIN-MODULE.
12        OPEN INPUT PAY-MASTER-FILE
13             OUTPUT REPORT-OUT.
14        PERFORM 200-INITIALIZATION.
15        PERFORM 300-PROCESS-RECORDS
16             UNTIL MORE-RECORDS = "NO".
17        CLOSE PAY-MASTER-FILE
18             REPORT-OUT.
19        STOP RUN.
20
     200-INITIALIZATION.
          ACCEPT RUN-DATE FROM DATE.
          STRING MM "-" DD "-" YY
               DELIMITED BY SIZE
               INTO HEADER-DATE.
```

FIGURE D.2   *COBOL Program continued*

COBOL CODING FORM

| PROGRAM | | REQUESTED BY | PAGE 4 OF 5 |
| PROGRAMMER | | DATE | IDENT. 73   80 |

PAGE NO.	LINE NO.	A	B

```
01          READ PAY-MASTER-FILE INTO MASTER-IN
02              AT END MOVE "NO" TO MORE-RECORDS.
03          PERFORM 400-PAGE-HEADERS.
04    300-PROCESS-RECORDS.
05          IF LINE-COUNT > 50
06              PERFORM 400-PAGE-HEADERS
07          END-IF
08          MOVE SPACE TO DETAIL-LINE.
09          MOVE NAME TO DL-NAME.
10          MOVE EMPID TO DL-EMPID.
11          MOVE DEPTNO TO DL-DEPTNO.
12          MOVE MONSAL TO DL-MONSAL.
13          WRITE REPORT-RECORD FROM DETAIL-LINE
14              AFTER ADVANCING 1 LINE.
15          ADD 1 TO LINE-COUNT.
16          READ PAY-MASTER-FILE INTO MASTER-IN
17              AT END MOVE "NO" TO MORE-RECORDS.
```

COBOL CODING FORM

| PROGRAM | | REQUESTED BY | PAGE 5 OF 5 |
| PROGRAMMER | | DATE | IDENT. 73   80 |

PAGE NO.	LINE NO.	A	B

```
01    400-PAGE-HEADERS.
02          ADD 1 TO PAGE-COUNT.
03          MOVE PAGE-COUNT TO PAGE-NUMBER.
04          WRITE REPORT-RECORD FROM HEADER-1
05              AFTER ADVANCING PAGE.
06          WRITE REPORT-RECORD FROM HEADER-2
07              AFTER ADVANCING 2 LINES.
08          WRITE REPORT-RECORD FROM HEADER-3
09              AFTER ADVANCING 2 LINES.
10          MOVE SPACE TO REPORT-RECORD.
11          WRITE REPORT-RECORD AFTER ADVANCING 1 LINE.
12          MOVE 6 TO LINE-COUNT.
```

The AS/400 allows COBOL to copy an external file description of a record into COBOL. The variable names used in COBOL are those entered into the physical file description, with the COLHDG text changed to a comment. The data type of A is converted to a COBOL picture of X, and the data type of S is converted to a COBOL picture of S9.

Enter the program as shown in Figure D.2. While you are entering the source member code, remember that you can save the code at any time by entering SAVE on the SEU command line. The Save command is considerably faster than pressing F3 and changing the Return to editing to Yes.

When you have completed entering the program, press F3 to exit and save your work. You will return to the **Work with Members Using PDM** screen.

COMPILING A COBOL PROGRAM

You are now ready to compile the report program.

Type	14	in the option column for the PAYB01 member
Press	Enter	

You receive a message for a normal or abnormal compile. When a program compiles correctly, an object will be created in your library with a type of *PGM and an attribute of CBL. The compiler output listing (found in your output queue) should contain no serious error messages.

If you have compiler errors, refer to the section on split-screen editing in Appendix C.

There are two methods to execute this COBOL program. The first is

Type	call payb01	on any command line
Press	Enter	

The second method is to access the **Work with Objects Using PDM** screen.

Type	16	in the option column for PAYB01
Press	Enter	

Both methods accomplish the same task, executing the COBOL program. To view this program's output, access your output queue and display and/or print the spooled file named QPRINT.

If you encounter a run time error, refer to Appendix F for error handling.

A Sample
RPG Program

INTRODUCTION

The following sections give instructions for entering RPG/400 source code to create a program to list the Payroll Master File that was created in Chapters 6 and 7. Remember that the instructions for using SEU are in Appendix B, and more information on entering and compiling source members is in Appendix C.

ENTERING AN RPG/400 SOURCE MEMBER

RPG instructions will now be entered for a program to print the Payroll Master (PAYMST) data. The program source member name will be PAYR01. The name is derived from the following abbreviations:

PAY (PAYMST file)
R (an RPG program)
01 (the first RPG program for the PAYMST file)

Access the **Work with Objects Using PDM** menu. You need to create an RPG source member. F6 is the Create command. This command will create a member and transfer you to SEU.

Press	F6	to create the new RPG member

The **Start Source Entry Utility** menu will be displayed on the screen.

The five entries on the screen are required by the Create function to place the program within your library and within the SOURCE file. The program will have a type of RPG and a program description.

Type	PAYRO1	for the source member name
Press	Field Exit	
Type	RPG	for the source type
Press	Field Exit	
Type	Payroll Master File Report	for the description

Compare the entries with Figure E.1. When all of the entries are as shown,

Press	Enter

```
                  Start Source Entry Utility (STRSEU)

 Type choices, press Enter.

 Source file  . . . . . . . . . > SOURCE        Name, *PRV
   Library  . . . . . . . . . . >   YOURNAME    Name, *LIBL, *CURLIB, *PRV
 Source member  . . . . . . . .   PAYRO1        Name, *PRV, *SELECT
 Source type  . . . . . . . . .   rpg           Name, *SAME, BAS, BASP, C...
 Text 'description'  . . . . . .   Payroll Master File Report




                                                                  Bottom
 F3=Exit   F4=Prompt   F5=Refresh   F12=Cancel   F13=How to use this display
 F24=More keys
```

FIGURE E.1   Start Source Entry Utility for RPG Program

The SEU Edit screen is now displayed.

Press	Enter	to compress blank lines and position the cursor
Type	IP	in the sequence number area of the Beginning of data line
Press	Enter	

The AS/400 will automatically display the H prompt on the lower portion of the screen as the first line of the RPG program. RPG/400 does not need the H spec; therefore display all possible prompt formats. Some of the RPG formats will provide prompt formats for *every field* shown on the appropriate coding forms. Some entries are partial field lists. For example, the J prompt is used for the input fields of an I spec, and the P prompt is for output fields of an O spec. Select any prompt as needed.

Press	F23	to display all prompts
Type	F	for the F spec
Press	Enter	

Using this information, key the program from Figure E.2, using the F23 key and the different prompts as required. Be sure to change all occurrences of YOURNAME to your userid.

While you are entering the source member code shown in Figure E.2, remember that you can save the code at any time by entering SAVE on the SEU command line. The SAVE command is considerably faster than pressing F3 and changing the Return to Editing to Yes.

FIGURE E.2   **RPG Program**

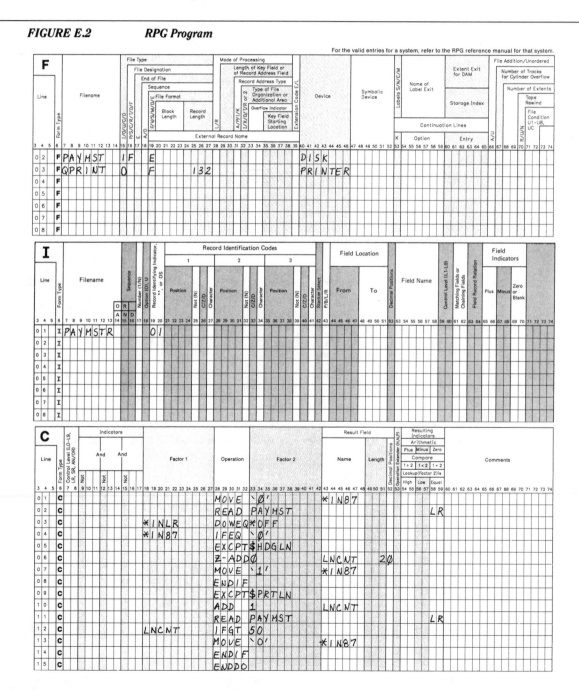

FIGURE E.2 **RPG Program continued**

IBM International Business Machines Corporation   **RPG OUTPUT SPECIFICATIONS**   GX21-9090-4 UM/050*
Printed in U.S.A.

Line	Form Type	Filename or Record Name	Type (H/D/T/E)	Stk #/Fetch (F)	Space		Skip		Output Indicators				Field Name or EXCPT Name	Edit Codes B/A/C/19/R	End Position in Output Record	P/B/L/R	Constant or Edit Word
01	O																
02	O	QPRINT	E		2	2							$HDGLN				
03	O														8		'YOURNAME'
04	O														53		'RPG SECTION 1'
05	O																
06	O		E		2								$HDGLN				
07	O												UDATE	Y	8		
08	O														33		'PAYROLL REPORT'
09	O														49		'PAGE'
10	O												PAGE	Z	53		
11	O																
12	O		E		2								$HDGLN				
13	O														13		'EMPLOYEE NAME'
14	O														30		'EMP ID'
15	O														41		'DEPT NO'
16	O														53		'MON SAL'
17	O		E		1								$PRTLN				
18	O												NAME		20		
19	O												EMPID		29		
20	O												DEPTNO		39		
	O												MONSAL1		53		

*Number of sheets per pad may vary slightly.

COMPILING AN RPG PROGRAM

When you have completed entering the program, press F3 to exit and save your work.

You are now ready to compile the report program.

Type	14	in the Opt column for the PAYR01 member
Press	Enter	

You receive a message for a normal or abnormal compile. When a program compiles correctly, an object will be created in your library with a type of *PGM and an attribute of RPG. The compiler output listing (found in your output queue) should contain no serious error messages.

If you have compiler errors, refer to the section on split-screen editing in Appendix C.

There are two methods to execute this RPG program. The first is

Type	call payr01	on any command line
Press	Enter	

The second method is to access the **Work with Objects Using PDM** screen.

Type	16	in the option column for PAYR01
Press	Enter	

Both methods accomplish the same task, executing the RPG program. To view this program's output, access your output queue and display and/or print the spooled file named QPRINT.

If you encounter a run time error, refer to Appendix F for error handling.

Error Handling

The AS/400 has a special menu to allow you to easily work with several system functions. Several of these functions are very necessary to error handling.

To access this **System Request** menu,

Press	Shift/SysReq	for System Request

A dashed line will appear across the bottom of the screen.

Press	Enter	to display the menu

The screen shown in Figure F.1 will be displayed.

Selection 1 will allow you to sign on to an alternative userid. You are able to sign on to two active sessions from one display station or PC. Selection 2 will be explained below, in the section on ending a program loop. Selections 3–7, 80, and 90 will not be discussed in this text.

ENDING A PROGRAM LOOP

An interactive application program is looping when the Input Inhibit indicator stays on for longer than normal and the keyboard is locked. "Normal" will depend on what you are trying to run. Programmers usually have some idea how long it takes a program to execute. If you are new to programming, several seconds is the maximum length for short programs. Check with your instructor for the length of time it should take your program to execute.

To end the looping program, the previous request to the system must be ended.

```
                              System Request
                                                    System:    XXXXXXXX
        Select one of the following:

             1. Display sign on for alternative job
             2. End previous request
             3. Display current job
             4. Display messages
             5. Send a message
             6. Display system operator messages
             7. Display work station user

           80. Disconnect job

           90. Sign off



                                                                Bottom
        Selection
             —


        F3=Exit   F12=Cancel
        (C) COPYRIGHT IBM CORP. 1980, 1991.
```

FIGURE F.1   *System Request Menu*

Press	Shift/SysReq	for System Request
Press	Enter	to display the menu
Type	2	to end your previous request to the system
Press	Enter	

This is the *only* method to end your own looping program. The operator can also end a program that is looping.

ENDING A PRINTER LOOP

Always display output to be printed on the screen first so that no unnecessary or incorrect output is printed. However, if you accidentally send a file to the printer that should not have been printed, do the following.

Stop the printer so that no more paper than necessary is wasted. If you printed the file from the WRKSPLF menu, you will have a message for the print file that the printer is stopped. If you printed the file from the WRKOUTQ menu, the file is not on your screen and you must use the WRKSPLF menu. See Figure F.2.

Press	Stop	on the printer
Type	4	to delete the print file
Press	Enter	
Press	Enter	to confirm

When the printer begins the next print job, there will be a message asking to verify alignment on the printer. As a courtesy to the next student, print something else

```
                        Work with Printer Output
                                                  System:   XXXXXXX
    User . . . . . :   YOURNAME


    Type options below, then press Enter.  To work with printers, press F22.
       2=Change   3=Hold   4=Delete   5=Display            6=Release   7=Message
       9=Work with printing status    10=Start printing   11=Restart printing


         Printer/
    Opt    Output      Status
         PRT01
    __      QSYSPRT     Printer message (use Opt 7)








                                                                    Bottom
    F1= Help      F3=Exit   F5=Refresh   F9=Command line   F11=Dates/pages/forms
    F12=Cancel    F21=Select assistance level   F22=Work with printers
```

FIGURE F.2   Work with Printer Output with Printer Message

so that you have to answer the message. (If another student was waiting to print, the printer might already be waiting for the alignment answer.)

The printer may be displaying a message code of 68. Turn the printer back on.

Press	Start	on the printer
Type	I	to answer the printer message

PROGRAM RUN TIME ERRORS

Programs can have run time errors for many reasons, including the following: an input data file cannot be found in the library list, an input data file cannot be read because the programmer failed to open the file, a physical file description does not exist for a new output file, there is nonnumeric data in a numeric field. A nonnumeric character in a numeric field is called a decimal-data error and is often caused by failure to initialize a counter or accumulator.

When programs fail during execution, the display station user receives a break message. This is an inquiry message and therefore requires a response. A typical error break message states that a program cannot proceed because of a run time error and needs to be canceled. But before the system cancels the program, the user is asked whether a system dump is wanted. Figure F.3 is an example of an RPG program decimal-data run time error message.

Inquiry messages list the accepted response options (C, G, S, D, and F). By moving the cursor to the message and pressing the Help key, the **Additional Message Information** screen shown in Figure F.4 will be displayed.

```
                        Display Program Messages

Job xxxxxxx/userid/xxxxx started on 11/19/91 at 08:18:07 in subsystem XXXXXXXX
1600 decimal-data error in field (C G S D F).

















Type reply, press Enter.
  Reply . . .  _____
             _____

F3=Exit   F12=Cancel
```

FIGURE F.3   RPG Program Run Time Error

```
                      Additional Message Information

Message ID . . . . . . : RPG0907           Severity . . . . :  99
Message type . . . . . : INQUIRY
Date sent  . . . . . . : 11/19/91          Time sent. . . . :  08:18
From program . . . . . : QRGXMSG           Instruction. . . :  0000
To program . . . . . . : *EXT              Instruction. . . :  0000

Message. . :  RPG101 1600 decimal-data error in field (C G S D F).
Pause. . . :  The RPG program RPG101 in library userid found a decimal-data
  error at statement 1600.  One field did not contain valid numeric data.  The
  digit and/or sign is not valid.
Recovery . :  Enter C to cancel, G to continue processing at *GETIN, S to obtain
  a system dump, or D to obtain an RPG formatted dump.
Possible choices for replying to message . . . . . . . . . . :
  D -- Obtain RPG formatted dump.
  S -- Obtain system dump.
  G -- Continue processing at *GETIN.
  C -- Cancel.
  F -- Obtain full formatted dump.
Press Enter to continue.

F3=Exit            F10=Display messages in job log         F12=Cancel
```

FIGURE F.4   Additional Run Time Error Information

This additional information explains the meaning of the acceptable responses and directs the programmer to the line in the RPG source member (statement 1600) that is causing the error.

Respond to all run time error break messages by canceling the program without a dump unless otherwise directed by your instructor.

Type	C	to cancel without a dump
Press	Enter	

G L O S S A R Y

AS/400
Terminology

ATTRIBUTES

Objects have identifiers named "type" and "attribute." An object's type describes the content of the object, for example, a file of data records, a library, machine-executable code, or output queue. Attributes further define the object. An object with a type of "file" could have an attribute of source physical file, physical file data, or logical file. An object with a type of machine-executable code would have an attribute of the programming language (COBOL, RPG, and so on). An object with a type of output queue has no attributes. For more information, see the Glossary entry Objects, Libraries, and Members.

COMMAND LINE

A command line is an underlined area toward the bottom of a screen where instructions are entered. Many screens have a command line. To request assistance in selecting a command or for help in entering command parameters, press F4 (Prompt). Press F9 (Retrieve) to return a previously used command to the command line. By pressing F9 repeatedly, the operating system will keep restoring previous session commands.

COMMAND PROMPTING

Many CL commands need more information to execute than just the name of the command. A CL command should always be prompted because the defaults might not be what are expected. Type the command and press F4. The AS/400 will display a screen or screens that allow specific parameter values to be changed. This concept of using the F4 function key is termed "prompting a command."

CONTROL LANGUAGE

The AS/400 operating system, OS/400, provides tools to operate the system called Control Language (CL). Simple CL commands can by keyed on the command line to go directly to a particular menu instead of working through several levels of menus. More complex commands can be entered by prompting. See the Glossary entry Command Prompting.

Programs can also be written in the CL language. A CL program can assist application programs to run. A CL program can be used to run a succession of CL commands that are executed frequently.

CURSOR

The cursor is a blinking block of light that tells the user where to type an option or command. The cursor can be moved with a variety of keys. See Appendix A.

DATA DESCRIPTION SPECIFICATIONS (DDS)

Data Description Specifications (DDS) are used to define external files. The field name, field length, data type (alphabetic or numeric), and other record information are defined with a DDS. The data description specification definition is contained within the AS/400's built-in database system and is therefore independent of any program. The advantage of an external file description is that multiple application programs may utilize the DDS and process the data using the same record or screen description. The Source Entry Utility (SEU) may be used to create a DDS for physical, logical, and display (screen) files.

DATA FILE UTILITY (DFU)

The Data File Utility (DFU) is an AS/400 tool that creates a temporary or permanent program to enter or change the data in a physical file. DFU provides a fast and easy method to accomplish this task. In a working environment there would be very few DFU programs, since DFU has limited editing, error message capabilities, and audit trails.

DEFAULT

A default is a value for an option or parameter that is assumed by the AS/400. A user can usually override these defaults by keying over them with a new option or parameter. Based on a user's prior work, the AS/400 will often utilize the user's last option or parameter as the default.

EBCDIC COLLATING SEQUENCE

Every computer system has a collating sequence, which is the order in which it compares and sorts characters. EBCDIC (Extended Binary Coded Decimal Interchange Code) is used on the IBM AS/400 and IBM mainframe computers. ASCII (American Standard Code for Information Interchange) is used on most microcomputers and non-IBM mainframes.

The collating sequence determines which characters will be placed first for the purposes of comparing fields, selecting records, joining files, sorting records, calculating minimum and maximum values, and determining when a control break will occur. The EBCDIC collating sequence from lowest to highest is:

blank
special characters . + & % , and so on
lowercase a to r
~ (tilde)
lowercase s to z
{ (left bracket)
uppercase A to I
} (right bracket)
uppercase J to R
\ (backslash)
uppercase S to Z
0 to 9

A major difference between the two collating sequences is that in EBCDIC, numbers are greater than letters, while in ASCII, letters are greater than numbers.

INPUT INHIBITED

When a user enters a command or option on the AS/400, it might take the system a few seconds to respond. While the AS/400 is processing the request, it momentarily stops accepting more keyboard input. This condition is called input inhibited. It is noted to the user by an X on the bottom line of a display station screen or an II highlighted on the bottom line of a PC screen.

JOB DESCRIPTION

A job description is a collection of attributes that defines a job to the AS/400. The job description includes a user's job and output queue priority and an initial library list. A batch job needs a job description. If one is not specified, information in the user profile is used.

JOBS: INTERACTIVE AND BATCH

An interactive job is a communication between a display station user and the AS/400. In an interactive job, information is entered at a display station, the system processes the information and gives feedback, and then the sequence is repeated. When a user signs on to the AS/400, an interactive job begins. This job is active until the user signs off. Interactive jobs are not queued.

By contrast, a batch job is submitted to a job queue, and the system runs jobs from the queue as CPU time becomes available. There is no interaction between the user and the system after a batch job is submitted. Compiles and report programs are typical batch jobs.

LIBRARY

A library is an object that contains other objects. Libraries are normally used to group like objects. A library acts as a directory to other objects. Every object that is created is placed into a library. For more information, see the Glossary entries Library List and Objects, Libraries, and Members.

LIBRARY LIST

A library list directs the AS/400 to search a specific list of libraries in the order in which they are listed. When a user does not specify a library name for an object, the libraries in the list are searched. The library list would normally include the user's library, necessary system libraries, and other libraries that the user is authorized to access. The system will inform the user if it cannot find the requested object in the list.

The library list is identified on a menu by the value *LIBL. If a menu parameter is *CURLIB, only the current active library will be searched for a requested object. This active library would normally be the student user name library. To view your library list, use the DSPLIBL command.

LOGICAL FILE

See the Glossary entry Physical and Logical Files.

MEMBER

Some objects can have members. *FILE objects contain members that have the same characteristics as the object. A *FILE object with a type of PF-DTA is a physical file object. The *FILE, PF-DTA object describes how data is stored on the AS/400. This includes the record length, any keyed fields, and the access path. A physical file object is the record format. It contains one or more data file members or it might be empty.

A *FILE object with a type of PF-SRC is a source physical file object. A *FILE, PF-SRC object contains members that are source members. These members may be programming languages, Data Description Specifications for physical files, logical files, menus, or screens.

For more information, see the Glossary entries Source Members and Objects, Libraries, and Members.

MESSAGES

There are two types of messages on the AS/400: informational and inquiry. These messages can come from the system, the operator, application programs, or another user. Informational messages do not require a response from the user. Inquiry messages require a response from the display station user.

System messages and some application program messages will be received on the bottom line of the display. Break messages appear directly on the display and have priority over any work being done. Other messages go directly to the message queue.

When a message is placed into a message queue, the user is notified by a buzzer and/or a message waiting light on the display screen.

Messages are viewed with the Display Message (DSPMSG) command.

Messages are sent to another user with the Send Message (SNDMSG) command.

MULTIPLE-USER SYSTEM

Computer hardware and operating systems that allow many users access at the same time are named multiple-user systems. Users share system resources, and the operating system shares CPU time among users' jobs as defined by a job priority.

OBJECT TYPE

Object type tells the operating system what operations can be performed on an object. All object types begin with an asterisk. Any object with a type of *FILE contains other objects. The objects within *FILE are called members because each member conforms to the characteristics of the file. An object with a type of *FILE that has an attribute of PF-SRC (physical file–source) will contain source code members.

Other common object types include *JOBD, *OUTQ, and *PGM. For more information, see the Glossary entry Objects, Libraries, and Members.

OBJECTS, LIBRARIES, AND MEMBERS

Examples of objects are libraries, data files, machine-executable code, and source code for programming languages. Each object has characteristics that tell the operating system what the object is and how the object may be processed. Therefore anything created on the AS/400 is an object. There are system objects and user objects.

Each object is stored within a library. A library acts as a directory to related objects. Some objects may have members, depending on the characteristics of the object.

OPTIONS

Many menus have options in addition to function keys to perform operations. Options normally reference operations for individual objects listed on the menu, whereas function keys provide information about the display screen or allow the user to exit or cancel the menu. Typical options include copy, delete, display, and work with.

OUTPUT QUEUE

See the Glossary entry Print Spooling.

PASSWORD

Passwords can be as long as ten characters. The maximum number of characters is determined by a system value. A password must begin with a letter and can contain letters and numbers. If a password is forgotten, the Security Officer can reset it to the system default.

PC Support/400

PC Support/400 is an IBM-licensed program that provides terminal emulation and other features to a PC-AS/400 connection. PC Support software must be installed on both the AS/400 and the PC. PC Support allows a PC user to emulate an EBCDIC display station device, store PC data on the AS/400, use printers attached to the AS/400 as PC printers, run PC commands while in an interactive AS/400 session, upload PC data to the AS/400, and download AS/400 data to a PC.

Physical and Logical Files

A physical file on the AS/400 may be empty or can contain data members. A physical file is similar to a traditional file as it stores data. Access for a physical file may be in arrival sequence or keyed sequence.

A logical file never contains data. The logical file is linked to one or more physical files. A logical file allows access to data in a sequence other than arrival and allows combining data from multiple physical files.

Print Spooling

On a large computer system such as the AS/400, printed output is not sent directly to the printer. All output to be printed is directed to an output queue. These spooled print files can then be released to a printer at the appropriate time. (*Note:* SPOOL equals Simultaneous Peripheral Operations On Line.)

Programming Development Manager (PDM)

The Programming Development Manager (PDM) accesses the AS/400 programming tools. PDM will call other AS/400 programs, such as Source Entry Utility (SEU), Data File Utility (DFU), and Screen Design Aid (SDA). PDM will assist the programmer to work with lists of libraries, objects, and members and to perform operations without having to know a specific CL command.

Queue

A queue is a holding area. The AS/400 uses job queues, output queues, and message queues. The system stores these items—jobs, printer output, and messages—for later use by the user or when the system resources become available.

Refresh

If F5=Refresh is a function key option on a screen, by pressing F5 the information displayed will be updated. On some screens the data may be changed by the user or the system after it initially appears, and the current values are not shown. To see the new values, the screen must be refreshed. Exiting that screen and immediately returning to it does the same thing.

F5 may also set a screen or menu to its original values. This is helpful when a keying error has been made before the Enter key is pressed.

RELATIVE RECORD NUMBERS

A relative record number is a sequential number beginning with the first record in the file. Record numbers are assigned in arrival sequence. The first member is always labeled as record one, the second record as record two, and so on. If records are inserted, the file is renumbered at the end of the session.

SCREEN DESIGN AID (SDA)

The Screen Design Aid (SDA) is an AS/400 tool to interactively design, create, and maintain online menus and screens. SDA generates Data Description Specifications (DDSs), which can be further manipulated with the SDA or Source Entry Utility (SEU).

SECURITY OFFICER

The Security Officer controls all of the security authorizations on the AS/400. The Security Officer assigns user profiles and resource security and can reset forgotten passwords to the system default.

SOURCE ENTRY UTILITY (SEU)

Source Entry Utility (SEU) is the AS/400 full-screen editor to work with source code members. Within SEU, records can be inserted, added, changed, deleted, moved, and so on. SEU provides line syntax checking of source statements.

SOURCE MEMBER

A source member contains source language statements such as CL, COBOL, Pascal, RPG, or DDS. The source member is within a source physical file object, *FILE object type, with an attribute of PF-SRC. For more information, see the Glossary entry Objects, Libraries, and Members.

SUBSYSTEM

A subsystem creates a suitable environment for a job to do its work. All jobs, whether interactive or batch, are run in an AS/400 subsystem. Each subsystem allocates main storage and other system resources to enable a job to load and execute. A subsystem assigns each job a priority, which determines how the job will be treated when competing for resources with other jobs within the same subsystem.

USER PROFILE

If the AS/400 security level is greater than Level 10, all users of the AS/400 must have a user profile containing the user's authority on the system. The user profile tells the system who can sign on and what functions each user can perform after signing on.

USERID

When you sign on to the AS/400, you must enter a user name (userid) to tell the system who you are. If the AS/400 security level is greater than Level 10, the userid is the name of your user profile, which was created by the Security Officer.

Index